WHAT THE DYING HAVE TAUGHT ME ABOUT LIVING

What *the* Dying Have Taught Me *about* Living

THE AWFUL AMAZING GRACE OF GOD

Fred Grewe

OPEN WATERS PUBLISHING

FSC
www.fsc.org
MIX
Paper from
responsible sources
FSC® C011935

Open Waters Publishing, 700 Prospect Avenue, Cleveland, Ohio 44115
openwaterspublishing.com

Printed in the United States of America on acid-free paper

17 16 15 14 13 5 4 3 2 1

CONTENTS

CONTENTS

For Lil' Bird and Eli . . .

■ ■ ■

I was afraid of dying, so I became a hospice chaplain. I figured if I hung around with Death, made friends with him—at a safe distance—I'd get used to him, and he wouldn't be so scary. So for the past nine years I have had the privilege to journey with more than a thousand folks who have gone on to the other side.

I've seen firsthand that no one escapes this world without experiencing pain, suffering, and death. It was a rather startling setback for me when this truth torpedoed my well-constructed life a few years ago. I had spent most of my faith-filled Christian years trying to do everything in my power to avoid pain and suffering. I'd been taught that if I prayed enough, read the Bible enough, lived a clean life, and volunteered to work in the church nursery once in a while, God would protect me from all pain and suffering. The thought that suffering could be good for me in any way wasn't even on my radar screen. But that was before I began to learn what the dying could teach me about living . . .

Preface and Acknowledgments

I GENERALLY DON'T TELL PEOPLE what I do for a living. I mean, when you tell someone you are a hospice chaplain they tend to just tilt their head knowingly and look at you with big doe eyes like you're Brother Teresa.

And I'm not.

It's not that I don't love what I do or am not proud of it. Actually I find my work both inspiring and refreshing. Inspiring because of the courage and strength I witness every day by patients and family members.

Refreshing in that I encounter very little in the way of B.S. By the time I get to meet our patients most of the nonsense has been kicked out of them—either by a doctor's terminal diagnosis or by some painfully failed therapy—or both.

Ministers by and large have to put up with a lot of B.S. I sure did when I was a pastor. It usually sounds something like this: "Why do we have to sing the same songs every Sunday?" or "You know, if we could just get out fifteen minutes earlier we could beat the Baptists to all the good restaurants," or "That was a wonderful sermon pastor, one of your best!" Pure B.S.

Hospice patients know they don't have time for such nonsense. Every alert minute takes on profound importance when you know there are precious few left. I find the brutal honesty of conversations with such people incredibly rich and refreshing. There's so little pretense, so little puffery. The sacredness of such moments demands my full attention and it feels as though time simply stands still in silent homage.

That's not to say such conversations are always serious. They're not. But what they are is honest. I remember when Carolyn was telling me about how depressed she became after her doctor told her that her cancer was inoperable and she only had a few months of life left.

"I stayed in bed for three or four days just crying," she said. "I didn't get dressed or shower—I just cried. Then one morning my daughter Jennifer came in and brought me breakfast. I started yelling at her that I didn't want any God-damned food and if I had a bag I'd just put it over my head and end it all right now!"

"Paper or plastic?" Jennifer asked.

Carolyn, with a big smile on her face, said, "Well, how can you stay depressed when someone treats you like that? So I got up and ate and decided to continue living until I can't anymore."

This book could not be possible without the incredible kindness and trust of folks like Carolyn. The access they allow me, a perfect stranger, to enter their lives at such a liminal time and share on such an intimate level is humbling. Any wisdom you gain from the insights in these pages is directly attributable to the brave patients and families I have had the privilege to serve over the past nine years. To them, I am incredibly grateful.

There are also others who have helped guide the growth of my chaplaincy and the process in putting this book together, and I want to thank them as well.

First, there's the men's group at the Ashland First Congregational United Church of Christ, who invited me to speak at our men's retreat several years ago and share what I've learned from working with the dying (the talk ended up becoming the genesis of this book).

My craft as a chaplain has been greatly shaped by my mentor, Scott Davis, and the chaplains of St. Louis University Hospital, who patiently taught me the care of souls. Today I share in this loving work with beautiful, caring colleagues (nurses, social workers, aides, volunteers, and clerical staff) at, first, Ashland and now at Providence Hospice in Medford.

I owe a deep debt of gratitude to my dear friend and writing buddy Michael Niemann, who has mastered the timely art of butt-kicking and encouragement; Doug Davidson, who molded my hodgepodge of random anecdotes into a real book; and Tina Villa and the unbelievably kind folks at The Pilgrim Press who have taken a chance on an unknown wannabe writer.

My sanity (such as it is) is nurtured by good friends Pastors Pam and Randy, Fathers Jim and Joel, Prakash (who is always up for an argument), and Luke.

Finally, I dedicate this book to my wife, Cyndi, and son, Elijah. Cyndi's search for truth and reality has led us both on a wonderfully unexpected journey and has liberated me from living a far too small life. Elijah, who genuinely makes me laugh, has taught me so much about acceptance—both giving and receiving. Their sacrifices to support our crazy lifestyle over the years cannot be tallied. I can only hope my living is worthy of their love.

> Lord, make me to know the measure of my days on earth,
> to consider my frailty that I must perish.
>
> —Johannes Brahms, *The German Requiem*

Prologue: The Test

■

Some people think we're made of flesh and blood and bones. Scientists say we're made of atoms. But I think we're made of stories. When we die, that's what people remember, the stories of our lives and the stories that we told.

—Ruth Stotter, *The Power of Personal Storytelling*

I COULDN'T HAVE BEEN more than five or six years old when I had my first awareness of spiritual things. It was a sunny summer day. A Sunday. I know it was a Sunday because we were at my Grandma Edie's house. We went there every Sunday after Mass for milk and cookies.

Something the priest said in the homily must have caused quite a stir because my parents and grandparents were talking about *heaven* and *hell*—concepts unknown to me. My folks tried to explain there was a life after this one. "When you die," they said, "there is a part of you still alive called a *soul*, and this *soul* goes to live in another place. People who do good things get to go to a place called *heaven*. It is a good place where God lives. It's safe and fun."

But there was another possibility. "People who do bad things," they said, "are sent to a place called *hell*. God isn't there, and those people will be on fire and in horrible pain forever. You sure don't want to go there."

This information struck at the deepest part of my still-forming little neurotic self. The world wasn't safe. I can remember walking down Grandma Edie's sidewalk after we left her house, feeling like I'd been punched in the gut. Life is a test. God is watching and keeping score. What we do, the choices we make, are really important. This thought burst the whole bubble of my young life. I realized living wasn't just about waking up in the morning and looking for ways to have fun. Life was a trial, and God was the judge. What a rotten turn of events. Deep down I'd always suspected the life I'd known was too good to be true, and now my worst fears were confirmed.

That morning marked the beginning of my spiritual journey.

I wish I could tell you my path since then has been a steady ascent into a blissful, peaceful state and I'm simply waiting around for canonization into sainthood. But you wouldn't believe me. Nor should you.

Truth is, my own quest has been fraught with failure, fear, and indecision. The good things I have tried to do to gain points on God's scorecard have been average at best. And the bad things . . . well, perhaps they're not as awful as some I have heard about, but they are pretty bad just the same.

I've had some amazing experiences on my quest. There have been lots of surprises and many disappointments as well. But here's the most important thing I've discovered: even though I have devoted much of my life to trying to seek God, the deeper reality is that I have been sought.

It's kind of crazy. I have spent so much time looking for God—endless hours praying for God to show up, years of studying to figure out the secret code that causes God to act, a lifetime of activity I hoped would please the Sacred Other—only to discover God's desire all along has been to shatter my false notions and ideas about who God is so I could experience the Divine Mystery for real.

Through these trials I've also learned we all have the capacity to change our behavior, to grow wiser, to become more compassionate. Often this transformation springs up from the fertile ground of our suffering. Growth is not a guaranteed outcome of suffering, however; one can read the sacred texts and attend all the popular seminars yet still remain a spiritual tourist. I assert there is a mysterious *X factor* required for true soul enlightenment, and that X factor is grace. Sometimes, as the old hymn says, this grace is amazing. Sometimes it is awful. Often it is both.

I've learned the spiritual path usually takes a circuitous route. It's rarely a straight line. Think about Moses for a minute. If one were to follow a direct route, the walk from Egypt to Israel would take about a week and a half. Yet Moses' journey following the fire and cloud to the Promised Land took more than forty years. For the Other whom we call God, it seems the journey is just as important as the arriving.

So . . . this book is simply the rough reflections of a fellow traveler. I've written these down not in an attempt to shorten your own journey or tell you what path you need to follow, but to encourage you along the way.

You should know the book you now hold is not the book I'd originally planned to write. When I first sketched it out, I imagined a book in which I'd explore a series of spiritual themes by presenting fabulous stories of my insightful interactions with hospice patients. For example, I thought I might describe the time I shared with a patient who was struggling with forgiveness, and then dazzle you with my brilliant reflections. What I soon discovered, however, is people's lives don't fit neatly into preformed molds of meaning, and any attempt to force them to would be artificial. And I hate artificial. So the "how to" book I'd hoped to offer you has become more of a "how come?" Instead of a surefire map to a profoundly spiritual way of living, what you will find is an invitation to embrace some of the deep questions that have challenged me to live more wisely and compassionately.

VITAL SIGNS

My primary job as a chaplain is simply to sit and listen to folks who are living life on the edge. *Really listen to them.* Now, of course, I do other things. My boss recently asked me to write up my job description so the hospice board of directors could review it, so I came up with a list of my various tasks and responsibilities. But the truth is I basically listen to people. Listen to their joys, fears, hopes, regrets, shames, neuroses, wishes, fantasies, and more. And often what I hear, as people talk about their lives, is the story of their all-consuming attempts to be acceptable. Acceptable to the people they love. Acceptable to themselves. Acceptable to God.

How do we come to know, not just to believe, but to truly know in an intimately personal way that we are acceptable to God? I believe it is only through grace. Amazing, awful grace. And as a chaplain I'm always prospecting for grace.

Over the years I've been collecting assessment aids to help me in my search for grace. One such aid is what I refer to as "spiritual vital signs." If you've ever spent a night or longer in a hospital, you've probably experienced having your "vitals" checked. Now, "vitals" is hospital code for five different measurements of health, that is, *vital signs:* blood pressure, heart rate (pulse), oxygen saturation, respirations, and temperature. These five indicators help inform your doctors and nurses how well, or not so well, you're doing. During a hospital stay, a patient's vitals are checked quite frequently. Vitals give the doctors and nurses an indication of what is really going on inside the body. If the numbers look bad, caregivers know they must pay special attention or take immediate action to prevent further damage to your body.

In my work as a chaplain I've developed my own list of *spiritual vitals.* Like the physical vitals doctors rely on, the presence (or absence) of these qualities often suggests what is going on in a person's life at a deeper, unseen level. When these spiritual vitals are out of balance, a person is often at increased risk of doing damage to himself or herself, or others, as a result of spiritual pain.

Here's my list of *spiritual vitals:* forgiveness, acceptance, compassion, meaning, gratitude, humility, mindfulness, trust, peace, and humor. These are the qualities I look for in meeting a new patient to help me determine the health of his or her soul. Remember, these are only indicators, and my purpose in assessing them is to design a plan of care that might help alleviate the emotional or spiritual pain this person may be suffering. Not all terminal patients have suffering souls. Many are in much better shape than mine.

This list of spiritual vital signs grew out of my experience of accompanying more than a thousand people through the final stages of their lives. Like physical vital signs, these spiritual vitals are fluid, not static. These signs may go up or down on any given day depending on what's happening in the moment, just as a patient's blood pressure might vary. But what I look for are overall trends.

These spiritual vitals are not stages one goes through or rungs on some celestial ladder that must be climbed to attain a mystical life. Rather, they are deep qualities woven together in the fabric of our unique souls. They are interconnected, and each individual displays them differently. I have found trying to isolate them to be futile. And, remember, they are simply *signs*—indicators that a soul has experienced the amazing, awful grace of God and is able to give this grace to others and to him- or herself.

I believe these spiritual vitals are often very complex and best discovered through stories. So as one traveler to another, I humbly offer these accounts of what I've experienced as I've walked with people who are facing death. I've made every effort to stay true to the people I've met and to their stories. Minor changes have been made to particular identifying details to protect people's privacy, but the encounters I've shared really took place.

There's a wonderful line in the movie *The International* in which Wilhelm Wexler says to agent Lois Salinger, "Well, this is the difference between truth and fiction. Fiction has to make sense." This book is not fiction, so don't be surprised if some of what you read doesn't make sense. You'll also discover I'm not always consistent. I don't claim to be. I'm a mystery to myself—as each of us is.

As you read the following stories, think of them as snapshots in a narrative collage. Better yet, see them as facets of a beautiful diamond—each presenting its own particular clarity and offering a unique perspective on what it means to create a life that is spiritually rich. I've given up on trying to fit the stories together into a neat and contrived whole; instead, I trust they will work their magic on their own.

A significant by-product of the time I've spent with the dying is that I've grown less afraid of my own death. Companioning with the terminally ill has afforded me a front-row seat to the circle of life. That's not to say it's easy. Sitting with folks who are in that place of "no longer and not yet"[1]—no longer who they were but not yet born into what they will become—can be uncomfortable. I've come to see Death as the natural conclusion to this first act we call Life. My hope and prayer is that as you read these stories, you'll have a similar experience in coming to peace with your own dying—and living.

Petey's Lament

■

When we sit with a dying person,
we understand that what is before us is not a "problem to be solved"
but a mystery to be honored.

—Parker Palmer, *A Hidden Wholeness*

IT WAS ONE OF THOSE orangey-brown late summer evenings just before dusk in South Florida. We were sitting on barstools in Petey's kitchen. Our wives had just taken the kids shopping when he looked me straight in the eyes and said, "I've got AIDS."

Three words. Three tiny words that spelled death for my best friend and began my own decade of spiritual deconstruction.

This conversation took place in 1990, long before I became a hospice chaplain. I was a preacher then—an evangelical charismatic preacher. My wife Cyndi and I had moved to Florida to start a new church. In the previous ten years I'd helped start two other churches, and the plan was that I would stay and pastor this one.

Within that faith tradition, the pastor was the guy with all of the answers. Pastors were expected to study the Bible so well that they could figure out most any situation by applying a Bible verse that addressed roughly the same ground as the issue in question. Or, for the really tough problems, you would get the answer directly from God. Folks found this method particularly impressive.

As a traveling evangelist, I was God's answer man. People came to hear me preach because I had all the answers. Or so I thought.

"I've got AIDS." His words just hung in the humid Florida air. I could not respond.

Petey was the brother I'd never had. He was loud and funny. He loved to sing, and to cook, and to make you feel special. He was the kind of guy you could just sit down with and tell your secrets to. You knew Petey wouldn't make fun of you.

We'd first met Petey, his wife, and their three kids at a church conference soon after my wife and I moved to Florida about two years earlier. Even though we lived about three hours away from them, we became fast friends and visited each other often. Petey was a leader at his church, which was a sister church to our new church plant. Cyndi and I had come down that weekend because Petey had just gotten out of the hospital where he'd spent several weeks fighting pneumonia. Cyndi and Petey's wife had taken their three teenagers to the grocery to buy food for our celebratory feast.

"I've got AIDS," he said again, as he stared right into my frightened eyes.

Some twenty years earlier while on a church retreat I had been saved. Radically saved. I became a certified Jesus freak. Since then I'd studied the Bible (reading the whole thing at least six times), developed a life of prayer, and served as an assistant pastor and traveling preacher—but nothing had prepared me for this moment.

How could Petey have gotten AIDS? I asked myself. He can't be . . . Naw, that's crazy. He's got three kids, for God's sake. He must have gotten some contaminated blood somehow when he was in the hospital. Or maybe they used a dirty needle. I read about something like that happening once . . .

"I've got AIDS." He was still staring right into my eyes. "I'm a homosexual."

It was one of those moments when time stood still. I was frozen. The seconds seemed to last forever.

As Petey continued to stare at me, a flood of thoughts came crashing through my mind. At first, I was so mad I wanted to choke him. How could he do this? How could he do this to his family? To his church? To me? Then I was seized by grief, knowing my best friend—this man I loved like a brother—was going to die. Then images of Petey having sex with other men came into my head, which really freaked me out. And, all the while, he kept staring into my eyes.

Petey told me he'd been molested by an elder at his Pentecostal church camp when he was thirteen. Petey believed this experience had unleashed his secret life of homosexuality. He was a loving husband and the father of three teenage children. He was a leader at his church. But unknown to anyone was the deep, dark secret of Petey's other life.

As I say, I had been a born-again Christian for nearly twenty years and a minister for more than ten. Yet in some unexplainable way, I felt closer to Jesus than ever before during this conversation. The Spirit of Christ came over me. I got off of my stool. I walked over to my friend and kissed him on the cheek. I told Petey I loved him. I told him we would go through this ordeal together. We hugged and cried. Petey had been waiting for me to reject him, but the Spirit of Jesus surprised us both with tender mercies.

The next three years were horrific for Petey. He had a simple cough he couldn't get rid of. His immune system was too weak to fight it off. For three years he basically coughed to death. One of the insidious things about the constant cough was that it robbed Petey of his ability to sing. He'd had a beautiful voice and was so alive when he sang. Now he was always hoarse from the coughing and could speak only in a raspy whisper.

Over the course of those years, I watched Petey's body literally waste away. Petey had always been larger than life; he was a weightlifter and a health nut. I felt so impotent just watching his once vibrant body shrink around his bones.

Those years were filled with so many bittersweet memories. I was with him when he told his children how he got AIDS and about his secret life. The kids had never seen their dad so vulnerable. After the stunned shock, these teenagers lovingly embraced and forgave their dad as we all cried together.

Petey was with me at the hospital when our son was born. As I came out of the delivery room carrying Elijah, I will never forget the look on Petey's face. I handed my just-born son to Uncle Petey, and he tenderly held the infant. In those days, there was still a great deal of misinformation about AIDS. One of the strongest fears was that you could get AIDS simply by touching someone who had the virus, so AIDS patients were not only traumatized, they were also stigmatized and quarantined. Petey just stood there and sobbed as he held Elijah. I was privileged to witness the affirming power of the human touch, as Petey held our baby—so healing.

The Christmas before Petey died, he and his family were driving by our home on their way back from a trip. Petey was in horrible pain, so his wife pulled off the freeway and they came to our house. Petey believed he was dying, but he didn't want to go to the hospital; he wanted to come to our house to die. After a while, we realized the pain was due to kidney stones. Petey and his family decided to try to get home. I didn't want his family to have to watch him in such pain, so I offered to take Petey in my car and follow them home. As we drove down I-95 in the middle of that December night, Petey was screaming out in agony, "Oh, God! I'm so sorry! If only I could have made other decisions. If only I had made other choices! Oh, God, forgive me!"

I was crying too, watching him suffer in such awful pain. I screamed back at him, "Why did you let it go this far! Why didn't you get help! Why didn't you tell anyone?"

He looked at me and simply said, "I was afraid. I was afraid I'd be rejected. I was afraid they'd throw me out of church."

I was so angry at the insanity of it all. My dear hurting brother was afraid of being rejected at God's house, the house of healing and reconciliation.

During the rest of his life, Petey and I prayed often. He made his peace with God. He experienced the liberating love of Jesus. Surprisingly, Petey told me before he died that those final three years of his life, even as he was dying with AIDS, were the best years of his life—because he was free. He no longer had to hide. He was free to be honest. Free to be real. Free to know that God loved him just as he was.

If only Petey had experienced these things earlier. If only we who are custodians of God's house could learn to welcome all who are dying for freedom.

Accompanying Petey on his journey toward death and wandering alone through the insane desert of grief after he died changed me forever. My dogmatic beliefs and memorized answers to life's difficult questions imploded under the emotional pain. I discovered (to my surprise) that even in this dark night of the soul, faith is not absent—just different. It's not as nice. Not as sanitized. It screams, rails, and curses the violence of death. One day sanity will return; homeostasis will be enjoyed again. But until then, the prayers of lament are faith's voice in the throes of grief.

a lament for Petey

where were You
as the skin tightened over his bones
and his voice
his lyrical voice
turned into that cough of departure
his voice
his life-giving laughter
turned into that damned rattle of extinction

where were You
when that pipsqueak tv prophet
proclaimed
AIDS is Your judgment on queers, faggots
and everybody not like him

where were You
as he coughed
and coughed
and coughed
himself to death

where were You
couldn't You hear

where are You
as his wife and kids groan
the desolate cries
of loss and shame

where are You
as that cold bony hand of grief
issues from my bowels
and chokes the very air from my throat

where are You
can't You see

and yet . . .
and yet . . .

the third day cometh
when Your healing touch will soothe
and i will trust You once again . . .

Amazing Grace

■

I once was lost but now am found.

—John Newton, *Amazing Grace*

SITTING ON THE BARSTOOL in Petey's kitchen that fateful afternoon was a critical moment in my life. It started the process of my questioning long-held presuppositions about God, faith, and my call to ministry. Looking back, I trace my trajectory toward becoming a hospice chaplain to that specific moment.

The most pivotal event in my life, however, occurred nearly twenty years prior, on November 21, 1971. The Feast of Christ the King. The day I first consciously experienced *grace*.

I was just your average pimple-faced, fat, shy, insecure, sexually naive Catholic teenager who, having grown up in a small West Virginia town, now found himself thrust into the complexities of university life. It was my freshman year.

I was an accidental drama student. I say "accidental" because I'd never really planned to study drama. During my orientation to college life, I was told I needed to have a major. Now, I'd never given much thought to being a collegian. I'd only applied to one school, West Virginia University, upon threat from my father (who'd never had the opportunity to go to college). I took the SATs the day before classes actually began. So, as I stood in line to register for classes, I flipped a coin, thinking I might like to be a lawyer or an actor. It came up tails, so I signed up for acting classes.

As a kid, I felt so insecure about being overweight that I developed a sharp tongue as a defense mechanism. If I made fun of other people, I wouldn't look so bad by comparison—or so the delusion went. Because I didn't like myself, I feared others wouldn't like me either if they really knew me. As a result, I had no real friends. People were afraid to get close to me. Get too close and I would slay you with my tongue.

So I spent the first few months of my freshman year in college studying drama. I enjoyed acting—it was a lot more fun being someone other than me. Plus, there were lots of pretty girls around. One of the required courses for an acting degree was scene shop. The whole class consisted of building scenery for the school's theatrical performances. I was never any good with my hands—but it was a required course. One day, as I was cutting some two-by-fours with a power saw, a voluptuous young actress in a low-cut leotard walked by. Paying more attention to her bouncing bosom than to my boards, I pulled the power saw across my left index finger. Blood started spewing everywhere. It's not a great way to meet girls.

After several hours at the university hospital emergency room, I got on the elevator to head home. When the doors closed, I realized I wasn't alone. A Catholic priest was with me in the elevator car. I awkwardly said, "Hi." He was pretty outgoing, and by the time we hit the ground floor, he had invited me to attend a retreat at a local Franciscan friary the next weekend. As we parted, he said the magic words: there would be girls on the retreat.

Since it was a Friday, I decided to knock off the rest of my day (skipping three more classes) and went drinking with some guys I knew. After effectively anaesthetizing the pain from my throbbing finger and lonely heart with cheap beer, I overheard some attractive girls in the next booth talking about going on a retreat the next weekend. I wasn't very spiritual, but even I could tell this was a sign from God! So I went back to the dorm in a drunken stupor, filled out the paperwork the priest had given me, and registered for the retreat. I wasn't seeking Truth—just girls.

The retreat was unlike anything I'd encountered in my nineteen years of life. People were hugging each other constantly and saying, "Praise the Lord." College-age students were carrying Bibles around. A buddy I'd conned into coming with me questioned what I'd gotten us into. To make things worse, the cute girls I'd overheard at the bar were a no-show.

The weekend consisted of students sharing their own spiritual experiences with Jesus in lecture format, followed by small discussion groups. I found it all very strange. While I believed they had discovered something that seemed good for them, it was nothing I was interested in.

By Sunday morning I'd had enough. Another discussion group was about to begin, and I didn't think I could endure it. Miraculously, at that very moment, the priest from the elevator asked if I'd like to go to the chapel instead and pray. Happy for any excuse to avoid the dreaded discussion group, where I would be expected to self-disclose, I jumped at the chance. I figured I could pray silently and continue hiding my fears of being vulnerable. On the way to the chapel, another retreatant wanted to speak with the priest. So he sent me ahead . . . alone.

When I entered the chapel, I just lay down on the floor to rest. I really wasn't thinking about anything in particular when I looked at the Tabernacle (where the elements of Eucharist are stored). It was an unexpected moment of illumination, as if a light had gone on inside me. Somehow I *knew* Jesus was really there. In the felt holiness of the moment, I closed my eyes. A picture emerged in my mind's eye. I saw Jesus splayed out horizontally on the cross, ready to have the nails punched through his hands. From my vantage point, I could see the face of the nailer. It was me. I had the hammer in my hand. I was the one driving the nails.

I looked straight into Jesus' eyes, and he looked back at me. I'll never forget that look. It's been more than forty years, but when I close my eyes right now, I can still see that look. I see the compassion, the love—but most of all—the *acceptance.* Those eyes pierced into my being.

In that moment I understood that Jesus died for me. I was responsible for his death. Every time I had wounded others I had wounded him. He died in my place. He died for me.

Another image flashed into my mind. Again, it was Jesus on the cross, but this time the picture was very much like Salvador Dali's Christ of St. John of the Cross. I felt as if I were somewhere in space, looking down on Jesus as he hung there, suspended with the whole earth beneath him. I realized Jesus had died for not just me—but for everyone. He died to save us all.

I started crying. I was overwhelmed. I had the sensation of my scalp being peeled back like a sardine tin while forgiveness washed over me and love poured into me. I was shaking and crying. I remember praying, "Jesus, I don't love you. I don't even know you. But if you teach me about yourself, I'll give myself to you. If you can make anything good come out of my life, I will live it for you."

At this point the priest entered the chapel and knelt down next to me. With some concern in his voice, he asked what was going on and if I would like to pray aloud with him. I did. He led me in a prayer to give my life to Christ. Some call this being "born again." Some call it conversion. My favorite writer, Brennan Manning, calls it being seized by "the Great Affection."

I don't know how long I stayed in the chapel, "skinny-dipping in the pool of grace," as a friend of mine likes to say. But I remember that eventually all the other retreatants came in for Mass. And I remember we sang "Amazing Grace." Of course, I'd heard the song before; as a disc jockey at a local radio station, I'd played Judy Collins's version—it was a Top 40 hit. But that Sunday afternoon I felt as though I were hearing the song for the first time. In that moment, I understood the words with the totality of my being.

Amazing Grace how sweet the sound
That saved a wretch like me.
I once was lost but now am found.
Was blind, but now I see.

For the first time in my life I experienced acceptance, total acceptance—blemishes and all—by the great Someone who knew all about me. The One from whom I could never hide.

The tragic irony is that, after experiencing the *amazing grace* of acceptance that afternoon in meeting Jesus, for the next twenty years I became a willing participant in the my-way-is-the-only-way-to-God legalism—a legalism *unaccepting* of anyone who was different from me and who didn't share my spiritual experience.

Mercifully, by traveling the road to death with my friend Petey, God's *awful grace* would begin to help liberate me from this religious blindness.

GOOD GRIEF

■

O Friend! There is a treasure in your heart. It is heavy with child.

Like trusted midwives, all the awakened ones are saying,

"Welcome this pain!"

It opens the dark passage of grace.

—Rumi

THOSE THREE YEARS JOURNEYING toward death with Petey and his family changed my life. The pain of watching my friend die a horrible death and being impotent to do anything about it unleashed unanswerable questions into my well-ordered theological world. My suffering shattered the idol I had made out of my far-too-tiny concept of God. I'd thought I had God figured out. I'd made a living out of teaching others what God likes, whom God likes, and what to do to become someone God likes. All that began to unravel with Petey's dying.

At the same time those three years pulled a kindness and sensitivity out of me I didn't know I had. I became a better human being by traveling with Petey on his road to death. While I would never have volunteered for the journey, I would not want to be the person I was before that experience. That's the paradox grief offers.

Grief is ugly, messy, and merciless. It reaches up from our bowels and shatters the illusion that we are in control of our lives. It takes us—against our will—dangerously close to the frontier of insanity; yet at the same time it is the fertile soil where a whole new way of seeing and experiencing life can take root.

One of the basic premises of this book is that our suffering can sometimes be the doorway to a much richer way of living—a life with more compassion and wisdom. Of course, there's no guarantee that suffering will lead to greater wisdom and compassion, but it is a real possibility.

Numerous faith traditions testify to this reality. One of my heroes, Francis of Assisi, experienced drastic change in his life after a near-death experience and protracted recovery from illness. Francis was converted from a self-centered, materialistic, pleasure seeker to an other-centered, spiritually minded saint. Ignatius of Loyola, who helped found the Jesuits, also had his spiritual awakening after a near-death experience. Zen Buddhist masters of the Rinzai school work with the help of *koans* (illogical questions) to bring their disciples to the point of mental collapse in the hopes that *satori* (an awakening) will take place.[2] Ascetics around the world willingly go to the edges of their emotional, psychological, and physical limits in the hope of experiencing an awakening, salvation, self-actualization, enlightenment—call it what you will. Native Americans go to sweat lodges on vision quests. Sufis become whirling dervishes. It seems many of us want more from life than just working at tedious jobs in order to make money to buy things that don't make us happy or fulfilled. Too many people spend their lives in such pursuits, only to wake up forty years later and face the uncomfortable questions: What is life all about? Why am I here?

For most of us living in North America at the dawn of the third millennium, the most common type of suffering we experience is grief. There are certainly other causes of suffering, some even more painful, but grief is one form of suffering common to us all.

Grief can be a doorway to this changed life experience—this moment of *light*—or it can simply make us mean and bitter. I have met, worked with, and prayed for so many people who have been sabotaged by the insidious feelings of "Why me?" "This isn't fair!" and "I don't deserve this!" These sentiments, while common and even necessary in the short term, are often destructive over the long haul. If we remain stuck in such places, we may find that our spirits shrivel and our souls atrophy until we become self-centered caricatures of living beings. Sadly, well-meaning but insensitive religious people too often magnify the pain of this living death with tactless comments or seemingly pious platitudes.

So what makes the difference? What causes the experience of grief to be a source of enlightenment leading to a more fulfilled life for some people, while for others it is simply a knife piercing the soul and leaving behind a breathing corpse of an existence? Although some spiritual guides assert with certainty that our attitude is what makes the difference, I'm not so sure. I agree that the individual's attitude is important, particularly in regard to choices like forgiveness and surrender (more about these later). But I have also seen where the demand that folks should "buck up" in a time of grief can lead to feelings of shame and guilt when they are unable to "put on a happy face." Often, out of our own discomfort with uncontrolled raw emotional pain, we commit spiritual abortion by trying to fix others and make them feel better before they are ready to be reborn into new life.

Trying to hurry ourselves or others through the grieving process is much like the story of the butterfly in Zorba the Greek:

> One morning . . . I discovered a cocoon in the bark of a tree, just as the butterfly was making a hole in its case and preparing to come out. I waited a while, but it was too long in appearing and I was impatient. I bent over it and breathed on it to warm it. I warmed it as quickly as I could and the miracle began to happen before my eyes, faster than life. The case opened, the butterfly started slowly crawling out and I shall never forget my horror when I saw how its wings were folded back and crumpled; the wretched butterfly tried with its whole trembling body to unfold them. Bending over it I tried to help it with my breath. In vain. It needed to be hatched out patiently and the unfolding of the wings should be a gradual process in the sun. Now it was too late. My breath forced the butterfly to appear, all crumpled, before its time. It struggled desperately and, a few seconds later, died in the palm of my hand.
>
> That little body is, I do believe, the greatest weight I have on my conscience. For I realize today that it is a mortal sin to violate the great laws of nature. We should not hurry, we should not be impatient, but we should confidently obey the eternal rhythm.[3]

The fact is, grief must have its way, and its way is different for every person. Often it takes its own sweet time. The process cannot be rushed. We human beings are very complex; we react differently in similar situations. There is no one-size-fits-all solution to the problem and opportunity of grief.

GRIEF IS HELL

It's not too often I'm called back into the hospital after the end of my workday. But when I am, it's never good.

The charge nurse on the other end of the phone was frantic. A baby had just died in the emergency room, and I need to be there *now*.

The automatic doors of the emergency department opened before me with a characteristic swoosh—and I walked into hell.

The beautiful young mother, Olivia, stood in a corner tenderly holding her dead child wrapped in a swaddling blanket. As Olivia sobbed gently, her husband, Francisco, was writhing on the bed in the trauma bay, howling with grief. Francisco's mother, the baby's grandmother, was in another bay of the ER being monitored for high blood pressure; she was the one who'd found the baby dead in his crib at home.

The rest of the ER was in chaos.

After getting bits of the story from staff and other family members who were there, I went into the trauma bay to provide support for the shocked parents. Francisco and Olivia had been out Christmas shopping while Grandma was babysitting six-month-old Eduardo at home. He'd been sleeping quietly in his crib when Grandma, just checking on him, found he was not breathing. He was gone before getting to the hospital.

Walking into that trauma bay, I could feel the life energy being sucked out of my own body. Such deep, raw grief is like an emotional black hole swallowing everything in its vicinity. Words are useless. I simply hugged the two young parents, looked sympathetically at the lifeless child in Olivia's arms, and then quietly introduced myself.

No one said anything for a long time.

After a while, I encouraged Olivia to lay Eduardo on the gurney so I could escort her and Francisco to the Quiet Room. There were several reasons for this. One was to reconnect them to their assembled family so they could receive loving support. Another was to help them get some fresh air to breathe as they gradually absorbed the reality of their situation. And sadly, I also needed to help clear the trauma bay, since it would be considered a crime scene until the county coroner could arrive and determine the baby's cause of death. This is standard protocol for every hospital. It is also incredibly painful.

The next four hours seemed to go in slow motion. Giving these beautiful young parents space to grieve with their family. Checking in on Grandma, who was blaming herself for not looking in on Eduardo earlier. Providing tissues and coffee and food as needed. Standing by to serve while trying not to be intrusive. And caring for members of the hospital staff who were also deeply grieving. Eduardo had been born at our hospital and the OB folks on duty remembered him and his family. The primary nurse caring for the family had several small young children at home, so she emotionally identified with the situation. When Olivia's doctor arrived, she hugged the parents deeply, and there uttered from them all such a wail of lament that it felt like all the air in the ER was vacuumed out of the place.

We learned that, in his short six months, Eduardo had experienced several heart problems and had been to several specialists. I was relieved when the coroner determined the child's death was simply a tragedy. The specter of suspicion was dissipated.

Being in the presence of such raw grief is exhausting. Yet, when I got home, it took a long time to get to sleep. Images of Olivia and Francisco and Grandma—faces twisted by awful emotional pain and shock—did not want to go gently into that good night. But I am glad I was there. I'm glad someone was present whose sole job was to care for these young parents—to offer them space to grieve the death of their beloved son, to give them respect and dignity in the awful waiting for the examination to conclude, to pray that they would experience grace even in hell.

THE AQUARIUM

A piece in the June 13, 2011, issue of *The New Yorker* magazine called "The Aquarium" by Bosnian-born Aleksandar Hemon offered an eloquently frightening window into the raw despair of grief. Hemon's second daughter, one-year-old Isabel, died after a grueling fight with a cancerous brain tumor. Isabel's grieving father writes:

> One of the most despicable religious fallacies is that suffering is ennobling—that it is a step on the path to some kind of enlightenment or salvation. Isabel's suffering and death did nothing for her, or us, or the world. We learned no lessons worth learning; we acquired no experience that could benefit anyone. And Isabel most certainly did not earn ascension to a better place, as there was no place better for her than at home with her family. Without Isabel, Teri and I were left with oceans of love we could no longer dispense; we found ourselves with an excess of time that we used to devote to her; we had to live in a void that could be filled only by Isabel. Her indelible absence is now an organ in our bodies, whose sole function is a continuous secretion of sorrow.[4]

Earlier in the article, Hemon wrote, "We stayed away from anyone who we feared might offer us the solace of that supreme platitude: God. The hospital chaplain was prohibited from coming anywhere near us."[5] As a chaplain, I fully understand his sentiment. There are times when no words of comfort are acceptable. As I share his story with you, I try to imagine what I would have done if Hemon would have let me sit with him. I hope I would have kept my mouth shut in the presence of such deep pain, put my arm around his shoulder, cried, and screamed at God with him.

I don't know if Hemon will ever experience enlightenment, or salvation, or if his pain from helplessly watching his daughter's suffering will ever cease. I hope so. But in no way do I want him to feel inferior or like a spiritual mutant if it doesn't. The truth is that there is no magic spiritual formula or amount of self-determination that can guarantee enlightenment. None of us can make an awakening happen without help from an unknown Source. It is only by the ineffable *awful grace of God* that our pain, grief, and suffering can miraculously become founts of wisdom and compassion.

Awful Grace

■

I need more grace than I thought.

—Rumi

On April 4, 1968, Bobby Kennedy was getting ready to speak to a crowd of political supporters in Indianapolis. As Kennedy was about to take the stage, a note was handed to him with the news that Martin Luther King Jr. had just been killed. In breaking the news to those gathered, Kennedy lamented the beloved civil rights leader by quoting the Greek poet Æschylus.

> He who learns must suffer, and, even in our sleep, pain that cannot forget falls drop by drop upon the heart, and in our own despair, against our will, comes wisdom to us by the awful grace of God.[6]

Æschylus wrote these words more than 2,500 years ago. They come from his play *Agamemnon*, the first work in the Oresteia trilogy. It's the story of how Agamemnon went to war to help his brother, the cuckolded Menelaus, recapture Helen (who had run off with a Trojan prince). To ensure victory and safe passage, Agamemnon sacrificed his daughter Iphigenia prior to the trip. This infanticide so incited Agamemnon's wife, Clytemnestra, that upon his victorious return from the war, she murdered him. With this telling of the insanities of war, revenge, murder, and adultery, Æschylus invented a whole new art form: dramatic tragedy.

In the midst of the emotional chaos depicted in *Agamemnon*, Æschylus's chorus poses those lines now made famous by Bobby Kennedy.

WELCOME TO REALITY

At the heart of these beautifully disturbing words is the question: Can anyone become wise *without* suffering? And the answer is a startling "No!" Æschylus is saying that no one can become truly wise (and I would add compassionate) without suffering. *No one* can become wise or compassionate *without suffering.* Somehow, mysteriously, in the perceived god-awful alienation of those never-ending pain-filled sleepless nights, our souls can be sculpted into something more beautiful. Zen master D. T. Suzuki has observed:

> For the more you suffer the deeper grows your character, and with the deepening of your character you read the more penetratingly into the secrets of life. All great artists, all great religious leaders, and all great social reformers have come out of the intensest struggles, which they fought bravely, quite frequently in tears and with bleeding hearts. *Unless you eat your bread in sorrow, you cannot taste of real life* [italics mine].[7]

Two profound observations by Suzuki help unpack the truth Æschylus is pointing at: suffering can enable us to live great lives, and the unique bread suffering has to offer is *real life*—reality.

Without denying *New Yorker* writer Aleksandar Hemon and the profound grief he has experienced, there is an alternate view to the role of suffering in our lives. Joseph Campbell, who made a career out of studying world religions and mythology, identified the nearly universal belief that suffering can be a doorway to heroic living. Campbell explained to Bill Moyers in their famous PBS interviews, "One thing that comes out in myths, for example, is that at the bottom of the abyss comes the voice of salvation. The black moment is the moment when the real message of transformation is going to come. At the darkest moment comes the light."[8] The biblical author of the letter to the Hebrews seems to agree by stating even Jesus of Nazareth was "made perfect through suffering" (Hebrews 2:10).

How does suffering transform us? By shattering the illusions we have inherited or created, and enabling us to see life as it really is. Living in reality is heroic living.

During my work as a minister, I have discovered another benefit to living in reality: it is there that we are most likely to bump into God. Christian theology has for centuries affirmed the belief that God is everywhere all the time. This concept, called omnipresence, is based in large part on the lines from Psalm 139:

> Where can I go from your Spirit?
> Where can I flee from your presence?
> If I go up to the heavens, you are there;
> if I make my bed in the depths, you are there. (Psalm 139:7–8 NIV)

But I have discovered one place in which God does not exist—in my fantasies. Because in my fantasies, I am God. The real God does not dwell in unreality. If we hope to encounter the living Creator, the only place this can occur is in reality.

Suffering alone does not provide such an awakening. Suffering provides the environment, the fertile soil, for a spiritual growth. But as Aleksandar Hemon and others would attest, suffering does not guarantee an awakening. Something more is required—awful grace. I suggest it is this awful grace that shatters our illusions, awakening us to reality where we can truly experience the Holy Other.

Awful grace is not something different from *amazing grace*—they are two sides of the same coin. Amazing grace is the experience of acceptance from the Beloved that encourages us to trust this Divine Other, even as awful grace painfully shatters our illusions and fantasies to awaken us to truth. The result is that we begin to live more heroic lives graced with wisdom and compassion.

Grace is not only amazing and awful; sometimes it's just plain *annoying*. Annoying because if grace is anything, it's personal. Intimately personal. Another cause of annoyance is that grace comes in its own sweet time. All the screaming in the world won't hurry it one bit. I've tried. But what's possibly most annoying: you can't earn it. It just shows up. Yes, it is liberating. Yes, it gives birth to hope. But it also requires change. Grace requires that I trust in God's loving acceptance and quit acting like a frightened little child.

Maybe Anne Lamott puts it most succinctly, "I do not at all understand the mystery of grace—only that it meets us where we are but does not leave us where it found us."[9]

TRAGIC HEROES

During my training to become a chaplain, one of the more formative books I read was written by a pediatrician, Margaret Mohrmann. In *Medicine as Ministry* she wisely observes that a patient's receiving a correct diagnosis is important, but what is more important is for caregivers to recognize that "this is a human being to whom a terrible thing is happening and whatever other name this terrible thing bears, its name is tragedy."[10] Dr. Mohrmann goes on to say that we are all heroes in our own tragic stories—tragic in the dramatic sense.

A dramatic tragedy starts with a character who is flawed, as we all are, yet exists in a relative state of harmony before all hell breaks loose. Events push the character to his or her physical and emotional limits; yet once the difficulty is overcome, the character is left in a much more balanced state of peace. Having experienced the tragedy enables the hero to become a wiser, more compassionate human being. And the hero is not the only one affected. For example, Petey was the hero of his story, and I was just a bit player—but like all great tragedies, even the bit players and audience members can be changed by them.

C. S. Lewis illustrates this experience of awful grace masterfully in *The Voyage of the Dawn Treader* (from the Chronicles of Narnia series). "There was a boy called Eustace Clarence Scrubb, and he almost deserved it," Lewis begins.[11] Eustace is a spoiled, priggish little boy, who is demanding and patronizing to all his companions. When the *Dawn Treader* harbors at a small island, instead of joining the company to help forage for food or firewood, Eustace goes off in search of fun. Stumbling upon the lair of a dragon, he discovers a den full of priceless treasures. Motivated by greed, Eustace steals a beautiful bracelet and puts it on his arm. But later, after he has fallen asleep, he awakens to discover that he magically has been turned into a dragon himself.

As a dragon, Eustace terrifies all his traveling companions, even though he tries very hard to make nice. This frightened little boy is liberated from the dragon experience only by the intervention of the lion Aslan (the Christ-like character). Here's how the boy recounts his transformation as the great lion used his claws of awful grace to tear away the dragon skin:

> The very first tear he made was so deep that I thought it had gone right into my heart. And when he began pulling the skin off, it hurt worse than anything I've ever felt. The only

> thing that made me able to bear it was just the pleasure of feeling the stuff peeled off. You know—if you've ever picked the scab of a sore place. It hurts like billy-oh but it is such fun to see it come away. . . .
>
> Well, he peeled the beastly stuff right off—just as I'd thought I'd done it myself the other three times, only they hadn't hurt—and there it was lying on the grass: only ever so much thicker, and darker, and more knobbly looking than the others had been. And there was I as smooth and soft as a peeled switch and smaller than I had been. Then he caught hold of me—I didn't like that much for I was very tender underneath now that I'd no skin on—and threw me into the water. It smarted like anything but only for a moment. After that it became perfectly delicious and as soon as I started swimming and splashing I found that all the pain had gone from my arm. And then I saw why. I'd turned into a boy again.[12]

As Lewis so beautifully illustrates, God's amazing grace is also *awful*—because God's merciful work of liberating us from our false selves often hurts like hell.

Like Eustace Clarence Scrubb, we all have created false selves to present to the world, hiding the frightened little child aching for acceptance underneath. Many philosophers and theologians have observed that the crafting of this false self is a universal response to the fears and wounds of life. We create elaborate masks made out of what we know, whom we know, and how much money and power we wield, all to hide our true selves. Like Adam and Eve in the archetypical story from Genesis, we're frightened—so we hide from God, from one another, and from ourselves. In this state we live shallow, hypocritical lives. In fact, the word "hypocrite" derives from an ancient Greek theatrical term for one who wears a mask.

The unmasking of one's true self is almost always painful. But it is also the only way to experience authentic relationships with God, one another, and ourselves. Awful grace is the way God frees us from this masked false self, freeing us to live in reality.

Like Eustace, we wake up to discover we are acting like dragons—and we begin to ache for liberation. Hence, amazing awful grace.

Joseph Campbell adds a wonderful insight about dragons from his study of mythology:

> But the dragon of our Western tales tries to collect and keep everything to himself. In his secret cave he guards things: heaps of gold and perhaps a captured virgin. He doesn't know what to do with either, so he just guards and keeps. There are people like that, and we call them creeps. They just glue themselves to you and hang around and try to suck out of you their life.[13]

The amazing awful grace of God comes to help us become less creepy and more human. Grace can liberate us from the greedy dragon of our false selves and enable us to become wiser, more compassionate people. But, as Æschylus warns, this awful grace usually comes to us against our wills. Against our wills because, given our druthers, we would all decline this life-changing experience.

Kiss the Son

■

When you've been broken, broken to pieces . . .

And your heart begins to faint 'cause you don't understand . . .

—Kevin Prosch, "Kiss the Son"

It's amazing how hearing an old song can bring you back to a particular time and place in an instant—years and miles traveled at warp speed by emotional muscle memory. Earlier today I was listening to "Kiss the Son," an old worship song by Christian artist Kevin Prosch,[14] and there I was back in the Middle-of-Nowhere, Argentina.

It was 1996, and I was totally unprepared for what would become one of my more dramatic encounters with God's awful grace. I was traveling as part of a ministry team on an eighteen-day mission trip to Chile and Argentina. The team was led by my friend Randy, who is a healing evangelist. Moments after landing in Santiago, we were taken to a big Pentecostal conference with about five thousand folks crammed into a large indoor arena designed to seat four thousand. I remember it was hot—Tarzan hot—and we were dead tired after a sleepless all-night flight from Miami.

We got there just in time for my friend to start preaching. He spoke for about an hour, telling stories of miraculous healings, before he launched into "ministry time." After he called for the Holy Spirit to come and begin to heal people, my preaching friend motioned for me to go pray for a lady who was seated on the ground floor in the center of the arena. She was visibly shaking.

As I made my way to her seat, I was feeling rather full of myself. I walked in a way that I hoped would communicate to the five thousand Spirit-filled attendees: "I'm part of the ministry team. The preacher is my friend. He sent me to pray for someone because I'm an anointed man of God." You get the picture. I'm sure you've seen arrogance before.

As I drew near the shaking lady, I was rudely awakened from my self-centered preening by what I first thought was a shaft of divine light. It turned out to be a reflection from the aluminum crutches she was holding onto. Oh, God—she has crutches.

All the faith drained from me in an instant. She has crutches. This was a hard one.

As I was contemplating how I would choke Randy later for sending me to this woman, I was shocked to see my own hand motioning for the woman to come out into the aisle. She lumbered up from her seat and made her way to me, using the crutches to drag her useless legs in front of all the folks seated in her row (they were the kind of crutches that clasp at the forearm). All this time she was still shaking quite visibly.

After she made it to the aisle, I felt at a loss for what to do. So I placed my hand on her forehead and began to pray. I usually prayed with my eyes open in order to see what, if anything, was happening while I prayed, but this time I closed my eyes. I was afraid of looking like a fool. We were standing in the center aisle on the ground floor of the arena where everyone, all five thousand, could see us.

After praying for several moments, I took a peek and saw she was really shaking now. Then, to my horror, I watched as my hands took one of the crutches from her arm and threw it to the ground. In my mind, I yelled at my hand, "What are you doing?"

My hand replied fearfully, "I don't know."

Miraculously, the dear woman didn't keel over. She just stood there, shaking hard.

I closed my eyes and continued to pray. I can't remember what words I prayed—probably something "in tongues" (vocal sounds intelligible only to the Holy Spirit), mixed with a lot of "Oh, God, please help." Several more moments, another peek, and then my hand did that crazy thing again, taking the other crutch and throwing it to the floor.

I closed my eyes again. Visions of the woman falling to the floor filled my mind. Everyone would see I was just a poser, a fake, a wannabe healer with no spiritual power. I was about to be attacked by five thousand incensed Chileans because I'd abused this dear crippled woman—and I couldn't even speak Spanish to try to explain.

I took another peek. Miraculously, the lady hadn't fallen over, and now it seemed her forehead was glued to my hand, or my hand was glued to her forehead. I was praying up a storm at this point. Not knowing what else to do, I started to walk backward away from the woman. But because her forehead and my hand were glued together, she started to walk with me, without the crutches—and then BOOM. It was like a bomb of faith dropped on the arena and all five thousand folks began to scream, jump for joy, and praise God shouting, "Gloria a Dios," as they saw the crutches on the floor and the woman walking with me to the front of the arena.

By now, I was shaking too. Truth be told, my shaking was more out of fear than anything the Holy Spirit was doing.

We continued walking like this to the front of the arena. I went up the stairs, and she followed. The whole place was in an uproar. My preacher friend was bouncing up and down with excitement like a little boy on Christmas morning who'd just gotten a pogo stick.

Once we were on stage, the master of ceremonies came over and started to interview the woman. I moved offstage and sat down, trying to collect myself. Amidst all the shouting, I could see the woman walking all over the stage and explaining that she'd been in some sort of car wreck and had half of her pelvis removed. She seemed to be in great shape, but I was nervous. I had no idea what had just happened, or how, or why. "Something spiritual" was definitely going on. I felt tiny. I knew God had done *something*, that I was somehow involved, and that it was holy. I was scared.

As I sat there on the steps of the stage all by myself, another dear lady came and knelt in front of me with a handkerchief, holding it out for me to bless like St. Paul in the book of Acts (19:12). I could only think, "Oh, lady, if you only knew who I am or what I'm like . . ." But since I spoke no Spanish, I just prayed over the handkerchief, then sat there and cried.

After this initial revival service in Santiago, we went to Buenos Aires, where we spent the next fifteen days in evangelistic meetings. Then our trip was to conclude with three days of services in a remote area of Argentina. By the time we reached Argentina, we were all very tired, but we remained excited. It had been an exhausting trip with several meetings and conferences each day, and we'd seen and been a part of amazing things.

The final meetings were held in a huge barn in the middle of a hayfield. The walls were corrugated tin, but you couldn't see them because they were covered with some kind of cicadas—the walls moved and looked alive.

The evening before the first meeting, a group of local pastors arrived to have a private meet-and-greet with my preacher friend Randy, so they could get to know one another before the conference began. Randy spoke to the assembled pastors for about half an hour and then asked if anyone wanted prayer. One pastor, a man named Victor, was in a wheelchair in the front row and requested prayer. After I was asked to pray with him, I learned that he'd had a stroke several years prior and was virtually lifeless from the middle of his chest down. Victor spoke no English, but his two children did and served as translators. We prayed for about a half hour with no results, and then it was time to gather for the evening rally.

The first night's meeting was a huge success. More than a thousand people showed up at the barn in the middle of the field, and there were quite a few healings, several from blindness. Randy and I prayed for an older woman who'd been totally blind for more than six years as a result of diabetes, and her eyes opened up in front of us. I'll never forget the image of her husband heaving with tears as he watched the event unfold. One of the event ushers who'd been blind in one eye since childhood was healed as well. Quite a night.

Before continuing, I think it is important to give some explanation of the events I've just related. When I use the word "healing" in this story I do not mean "cure" in any Western scientific or medical sense. These experiences were to my knowledge never verified objectively. But here's my dilemma. I saw these events with my own eyes. They actually happened. They helped form the person I have become. I really can't explain with any degree of certitude what actually took place from a medical or scientific or even spiritual perspective. I just know something significant was happening to myself and these folks—and it was bigger than us.

The next night Victor arrived early, but his children explained that he couldn't stay for the rally because he wasn't feeling well. A friend and I prayed for him for another half hour to no effect.

By the final night, I was emotionally and physically exhausted. I hadn't seen my wife and son in nearly three weeks. My days had been filled with meetings and conferences and praying for thousands of people who were all hurting in some way. But for me, the hardest thing was the feeling of always having to be "on." No time to just relax and do nothing.

We were about to sit down to the evening meal before the final meeting when some folks came to ask if I would pray for Victor once again. I was told he was in the small house next to the barn. While I wasn't willing to admit it, I was pissed. I was exhausted, and I'd already prayed for this dear man several times. I had nothing left in the tank. I was whining silently to God the whole way over to the small farmhouse. I was just worn out from acting like a Christian for three whole weeks.

They took me into the farmhouse and led me to a small bedroom filled with folks. As I entered the room, the people parted to make room for me to pass through, and there was Victor lying naked on the bed. "This is weird," I thought. When I got to the side of the bed, a missionary doctor was looking at a wound at the base of Victor's spine. The bone was coming through his rotting flesh, and the doctor was tapping the bone with a spoon. Victor could feel nothing but was shivering with a fever. I nearly threw up.

I had no idea.

I had no idea of how much Victor was suffering.

To me, Victor had simply been a project—a test for divine healing or supernatural power—and I didn't have direct access to either.

I lay down on the bed and held this dear man in my arms. I told Victor's children not to translate what I was about to pray. Then I started to scream like a wounded animal at God. How could a loving God allow such misery? In the three times I'd been with Victor, I'd never heard him complain or utter even the slightest hint of doubt. He was still working full-time as a pastor but couldn't even hold his wife in his arms. He was confined to a chair, a decubitus ulcer eating away the flesh on his buttocks, yet he was the model of grace and kindness. Insanity.

After about a half hour of tearful screaming rage at God masked as prayer, I went back to the barn to get ready for the evening service. I was still visibly shaken as I sat down to get a small bite to eat when Randy came in and asked me what was going on. I told him.

I could hear the music starting, and the evening meeting was beginning. Because of Victor's condition, he couldn't stay for the meeting so his friends and family had carried him to a small car parked in the hayfield and were going to take him home. The car had plastic wrapped around the seats so Victor's flesh and blood would not stain them. I was seated on an aluminum folding chair in a garage-door-sized opening at the back of the barn as I watched my friend Randy go out to the car to pray for Victor. It was a surreal scene that is forever burned into my memory.

Outside, in front of me, sat a dear little man named Victor who was in intense suffering, as my friend Randy quietly prayed for him. It was dusk, and the only light in the middle of the hayfield was the dome light of the parked car that shone on Randy's head as he prayed. Inside, behind me, the lights were bright. There was singing and dancing and shouting for joy as people celebrated the miracles from the previous night's meetings. Ushers were lining people up to give their testimonies of how God had so powerfully touched and healed them. There were even a few pointing at me, as if I were the superman of faith God had used to heal them.

In that moment time stopped for me. I sat on the chair in the barn doorway and cried, asking God, "How can all this be?" The word of the Lord came to me and simply said, "You don't understand. On one side of this reality is darkness and suffering and pain and questions. On the other is singing and dancing and healing and celebration. Between the two is a door you call death. And that's just the way it is."

Victor was not healed.

The musicians inside the barn began to sing "Kiss the Son" as Victor's wife drove their little Fiat off into the night. I was left to battle with uncertainty and questions I'd never had the courage to face before, all alone in the Middle-of-Nowhere, Argentina.

When the rock falls, falls upon you.
And you get ground to dust no music for your pain.
. . . Well, though You slay me, I will trust You, Lord.[15]

Sleepless in St. Louis

This is the most profound spiritual truth I know: that even when we're most sure that love can't conquer all, it seems to anyway.

—Ann Lamott, *Traveling Mercies*

My education about the opportunities grief affords in experiencing God's *amazing awful grace* was significantly furthered one night early in my chaplaincy training. It was about 10:30 when Ms. Benjamin called. "We've just had a full arrest here in the ER," she told me. "Full arrest" is hospital code language for a fatal heart attack. As the only chaplain in the hospital at that hour, I needed to go to the ER immediately to help comfort the family.

During that residency year of chaplaincy training, I worked a twenty-three-hour day every Thursday. It had already been a difficult night; this was the third death on my watch.

I could hear Ms. Benjamin was smiling. She loved to call me down to the emergency room for difficult situations because she knew I really cared for folks. She also knew I was terrified. Benji and I had become dear friends several months earlier when she told me I was "jinky." I had always been intimidated in the ER. Everyone was always rushing around on what seemed to me to be life-and-death matters. As a chaplain, I felt I was just in the way. No one ever talked to me. That was until that one hectic night when Ms. Benjamin just looked up at me and said, "You're jinky."

"What?" I said.

"You're jinky," she repeated. I understood she was saying I was bad luck. On the nights I worked, all hell seemed to break loose in the ER. In my most playful manner I looked her right in the eye and said, "How dare you call the man of God *jinky*! That's just bullshit." We'd been fast friends ever since.

I went to the ER the minute I hung up the phone. As soon as I got there, Stephanie from admitting came up to tell me the family was gathered in the Quiet Room. I loved the admitting folks, and they knew it. Whenever they knew I had to go into an awful family situation, they always had this little gleam in their eyes that whispered, "Better you than me." It's the dark humor that often keeps you going when working in difficult situations.

After Stephanie filled me in on the man who'd died, Dr. Ward and I prepared to enter the room. As the attending physician, Dr. Ward was responsible for informing the family that their loved one had died. Chaplains aren't supposed to give out any medical information, and since death is a medical condition, that's the doctor's responsibility. I was basically just there for emotional cleanup. Unfortunately, although he was a kind and thorough physician whom I really liked, Dr. Ward's bedside manner was a bit lacking. It seemed giving bad news always made him nervous.

We walked into the Quiet Room—a small, windowless, tile-floored cubicle furnished with cheap tubular institutional chairs. To really imagine the scene, you need to know that Dr. Ward, the patient who'd died, and the two women waiting for the news were all African American. I am not. I am white as snow. As soon as we stepped in, Dr. Ward said to the patient's daughter and auntie, "I'm Dr. Ward. Mr. Wilkins is dead."

They stared at us in utter shock. After a few gasping-for-air moments, the patient's daughter, Telika, ran out of the Quiet Room into the ER waiting room (which was always filled with sick people and their families). Her mother, the patient's significant other, had just walked into the waiting area, and Telika gave her the news. Monique, Mr. Wilkins's girlfriend, was very drunk. When Monique got the news about Mr. Wilkins, she started to swoon and scream at the top of her lungs in anguish. Two big young guys were with her and helped restrain her.

I quickly tried to usher everyone back into the Quiet Room, partly for the family's privacy but mostly to avoid causing all the sick people and their loved ones in the waiting room to freak out. When we got back in, Monique was still screaming, "Shit. Shit. Shit. What am I going to do? He's the only who cares for me! What am I going to do?"

Dr. Ward asked if the family had any questions, but by then chaos had taken hold. In the blink of an eye, another fifteen people entered the room—young children, teenage boys, and men and women of various ages, African Americans all. There were tears and words of disbelief, and Monique continued to freak out. A few moments later, after Dr. Ward gave his parting condolences, I was left alone in the Quiet Room with about twenty shocked folks, including Monique, who was still screaming and swooning.

Everyone wanted to see Mr. Wilkins's body. Now, the hospital had very strict rules of procedure for such events. Since Mr. Wilkins was lying in Trauma Bay 2 back in the ER, and there were many hurting patients and busy staff members between him and us in the Quiet Room, safety was an issue. The hospital allowed for only two visitors at a time, and they had to be escorted for security reasons. There was no way I could take Monique back to see Mr. Wilkins body at this time. She had to settle down first.

After explaining that I was a chaplain, I got her a cup of coffee and encouraged her to drink it. She asked for cream and sugar, so I went to get it. When I got back, Monique was crying very hard—tears swimming down her cheeks, snot oozing from her nostrils. She buried her fluid-filled face into my new dress shirt. (I must confess that, at that moment, I thought about the cost of the shirt and how I would try to get it cleaned. I know, not very spiritual.) Through her sobs, I could hear her mumbling, "Who will take care of me? He's the only one who loved me."

After several more minutes, Monique pulled it together and, with the help of two large young men, I escorted her back to see Mr. Wilkins. It was like a morbid, slow-motion procession: a couple of steps, a small swoon, a few more steps. I held Monique's left arm, one of the young men held her right, and the other young man was behind us to catch her if we dropped her. As we got about thirty yards from Trauma Bay 2, ambulance drivers were bringing in another patient on a gurney—so we covered the last few steps at a sprint, tied together like participants in a three-legged race.

When we turned the corner and pulled aside the curtain, there was Mr. Wilkins's body lying on a gurney. He was already becoming cold and stiff. He still had a plastic tube protruding from his lifeless mouth. Monique rushed over and threw herself on his body and began to kiss his head tenderly. I went to get chairs for everyone. Time becomes a nonfactor in moments like this. It just seems to cease to exist. The three of us just sat and watched this frightened woman grieve for the man she loved. A few moments later, Monique's daughter joined us. She was crying, too.

No one talked. We just sat in death's presence for a long while. The nurse eventually came to inform me that Mr. Wilkins's mother had arrived and other family members wanted to come back and pay their respects. Monique tenderly blurted out, "He was a good man." One of the young men said, "He knew God, that's for sure." The other man nodded in agreement.

Monique, still lying on Mr. Wilkins's body, looked up at me and asked, "Who are you?"

"The chaplain," I replied.

"Where is he now?"

"In a better place," I responded half-heartedly.

"Are you sure?"

"I believe so."

After a little while I left and began the process of running a shuttle service between the Quiet Room and Trauma Bay 2—escorting family members and friends back to say a final goodbye to Mr. Wilkins. After that important task was complete, I gathered everyone back into the Quiet Room. As you can imagine, it was a bit close in there. There was nothing left to be done, but no one wanted to leave. To alleviate my own awkwardness, I tried to wrap things up by saying again (for maybe the thousandth time) how sorry we all were for their loss.

Monique started up again, screaming, "Shit. Shit. Shit. I need to go wake him up. I need to go kiss him again."

I politely grabbed her and said, "We can't go back in there."

She yelled, "If he saw you people trying to stop me, he'd sit right up and say, 'Get your fucking hands off her! Leave her alone.'"

The whole family looked like they were embarrassed by Monique and her outbursts. She was drunk, screaming. Her daughter, Telika, wouldn't even look at her and curtly said, "Stop it mother! Be quiet."

I grabbed Monique to keep her from swooning again. "Shit. Shit. Shit." Then she looked at me as if we hadn't met and asked, "Who are you again?"

I was exasperated and said, "I've told you more than thirty times tonight: I'm the chaplain!"

She put her hand over her mouth in horror, as if to say, "I've just said dirty words in front of the man of God."

Everyone was staring at us. The embarrassment was palatable. Trying to ease the tension, I said with a glint in my eye and a smile on my face, "Well, this has been an educational night for me. I've heard the word "shit" more in the last two hours than in my whole life."

There was a brief shock-filled silence—then everyone started to laugh. I mean, *really* laugh. Dear little Mildred, Mr. Wilkins's eighty-year-old mother said, "I'm laughing so hard my belly hurts." Mr. Wilkins's church-going auntie (who had on her Sunday best, including a beautiful pink hat) bowed her head, raised her right arm, and was alternately laughing and saying, "Sweet Jesus, Sweet Jesus," and laughing again. The young men were laughing the most.

Monique looked at me in disbelief. I cupped her face with my two hands, looked her right in the eyes, and said, "Ma'am. It's all right. When my time to pass comes, I can only hope my wife will miss me as much as you miss Mr. Wilkins. It's all right." She started to cry again, and I tenderly pulled her head to my chest and just held her.

There are times when I think the best thing a chaplain can do is help create a safe place for people to go crazy.

One of the young men stood up and asked, "Chaplain, would you pray for us?"

"I'd be honored." I grabbed the hands of those sitting next to me and everyone stood up. We made a little circle, everyone bowed their heads, and I began to pray. "Father, tonight we ask you to receive Mr. Wilkins lovingly into your bosom. Jesus, you promised you were going ahead of us to prepare a room for us in the Father's house." (The church-going auntie was whispering, "Yes, Lord! Oh yes, Lord!") "So tonight please usher Mr. Wilkins into that room you have prepared just for him. May he dearly enjoy his eternal reward. And I ask for us that you would comfort us. Dear Jesus, one of the names you gave the Holy Spirit is the Comforter, because you knew there would be mornings when we'd need comforting. Well, this is one of those mornings. So, dear Comforter, please come and comfort those of us who are left behind."

One of the young men said, "Amen."

I stood by the door to say goodbye. One by one, as the friends and family members left, each stopped to give me a hug. The big young men, the little girls, the aunts, Mr. Wilkins's mother—every single one of them gave me a hug. Suddenly, I didn't feel so old and tired and white. For that evening in the ER, grief had opened the door for God's *amazing awful grace* to strip away the artificial distinctions we've created of black and white, rich and poor, young and old. It helped liberate me from my own racial biases and misunderstandings. It had apprehended us. It ushered us all into reality. It reminded us we were frail family members on this journey called life—human beings all.

Jack Shit

■

Man is a god who shits.

—Ernest Becker, *The Denial of Death*

I'd been in Jack's house for less than five minutes when he sadly confessed, "God can never forgive me."

Jack was very tall and lean—gangly is the word—and chronic back pain left him bent over at the waist like a twisted piece of elbow macaroni. His blue jeans looked three sizes too big and were held up precariously by bright red fireman suspenders.

Very witty, sadly charming, and warmly hospitable, Jack reminded me of an incarnate Eeyore from Winnie-the-Pooh. He was woefully forlorn and depressed—but in an endearing way. You just wanted to hug him. An avid student of the Bible and an active member of a local fundamentalist church, Jack was sure God could never forgive him.

"Wow," I said. "Can I get your autograph?"

His head snapped up from his rocking chair, and he peered at me with those dark, deeply set eyes full of suspicion. "What? . . . Why?"

"Well, I've never met anyone before who claimed to be more powerful than God."

"What do you mean?" he asked incredulously.

"Well, if I understand you right, you're telling me your ability to sin is greater than God's ability to forgive."

Jack stroked his long pointy chin for several seconds. Then, smiling, he sheepishly admitted, "I guess that *is* what I'm saying." We both laughed out loud.

Over the course of my visits with him, Jack shared about his life, his broken marriage, his love for God, and his fear of dying. He never did tell me what awful sin he'd committed that caused his spiritual angst. On one occasion, though, he did share a deeply painful memory. Jack told me that, as his father was dying, his father had told another family member that Jack had been a great disappointment to him. Jack and his father had always had an ambiguous relationship. Jack's dad had been a larger-than-life figure, a football star known not only for breaking tackles but also for breaking women's hearts—including the heart of Jack's "sainted mother." Jack both loved and hated his father. Jack longed desperately for his father's approval yet also feared he would become like his dad.

Was it a coincidence that this man who struggled for, yet never received, his father's affirmation would worship a God for whom he was never quite good enough?

Each week our hospice team of nurses, social workers, home health aides, a doctor, a pharmacist, and a chaplain gathers to discuss the progress of each patient to ensure we are doing the best we can for them. At one of these weekly meetings, Jack's nurse mentioned that Jack was obsessed about the movements of his bowels. The goal of Jack's day, she shared, was to have a B.M. As the nurse shared this quirk of Jack's behavior, I had a stroke of insight: *Jack can't let go of his shit*—physically or spiritually.

Somehow, during those months as Jack was dying, his thirsty soul was slaked by the waters of grace. Maybe it was as Æschylus portrayed, that God's *awful grace* came to Jack during those long sleepless nights when he lay awake perseverating about his bowels? I don't know.

But I do know that Jack came to a deep measure of peace before he died. Somehow he became convinced God really did forgive him. On my last visit with Jack before he died, he told me he wasn't afraid anymore, but he still prayed that God would just let him die one night during his sleep. I teasingly responded, "Jack, everyone wants that." Jack admitted that he was inconsistent—he wanted to die peacefully but he also wanted to do everything possible to stay alive. Jack taught me consistency is overrated. We're all inconsistent—it's simply part of being human.

Before he died, Jack experienced grace—the merciful, loving acceptance he so longed for all of his life. This somehow enabled Jack to finally let go of his shit and enjoy an important freedom—the freedom to die in peace. I can confirm that this was no small task. Sometimes letting go of your shit requires a herculean effort.

THE WAGER

According to the ancient Greek myth, one of the Twelve Labors of Hercules was to clean out the Augean Stables. King Augeas was the richest man in Greece at the time, the owner of thousands of head of cows, bulls, goats, sheep, and horses. Every night his workers brought the animals back to their stables, which had never been cleaned out. The pile of shit was legendary.

Augeas bet Hercules that he couldn't clean out the stables in one day. Hercules accepted the challenge and come up with an ingenious plan. He grabbed a shovel and walked right past the huge pile of dung—didn't even look at it. Instead, Hercules started digging a trench at the back of the stables in the direction of two nearby rivers, the Alpheus and the Peneus. When he released their banks, the two rivers merged and created such a huge surge of water that it washed all the crap from the stables, redistributing it to the depleted fields below that were in desperate need of fertilizing.

The moral of the story is that we sometimes find our shit so overwhelming that we simply can't get rid of it. So instead of endlessly shoveling crap, maybe it's a better idea to dig a trench to the source of grace, to that place of love and acceptance, and allow grace to flow down and wash away our filth. It might even become fertilizer enriching our life and the lives of others!

HIDE AND SEEK

My dear friend Jack had hit the trifecta: he had relational problems with himself, with others, and with God. Now, some would argue these are all one and the same. I disagree. I will concede, however, that these three are deeply interconnected and not easily separated. If we violate one of these three relationships, the others will surely be affected.

I suspect some of you will be freaked out if I bring up the word *sin*. And I understand: it does come with a lot of baggage. But one thing all the major faith traditions agree on is we human beings have a problem. Islam, Judaism, and Christianity call it "sin." Taoism and Buddhism teach that we are all asleep and need to be "awakened." Twelve-step groups tell us we have "imperfections." But these belief systems all agree that we human beings are not fully what we were meant to be.

In the well-known story from the Bible, we're told of how God's garden became polluted by the weeds of sin—the Bible's word for the soul-sickness that has infected us all. Although God commanded that the humans not eat from the tree at the center of the garden, the Serpent suggested they would not die from eating the forbidden fruit; instead, they would become enlightened. Then we read:

> When the Woman saw that the tree looked like good eating and realized what she would get out of it—she'd know everything!—she took and ate the fruit and then gave some to her companion, and he ate. Immediately the two of them did "see what's really going on"—saw themselves naked! They sewed fig leaves together as makeshift clothes for themselves.
>
> When they heard the sound of God strolling in the garden in the evening breeze, the Man and the Woman hid in the trees of the garden, hid from God. God called to the Man and the Woman: "Where are you?"
>
> He said, "I heard you in the garden and I was afraid because I was naked. And I hid." (Genesis 2:25–3:11 MSG)

What is Yahweh's reaction to this devastation of the Divine Plan? Does God come exploding onto the scene in scolding tones threatening, "Get out here you two! I told you if you ate my fruit I'd give you what for! I'm gonna squash you both like the ungrateful bugs you are!" Quite the contrary! In what comes as a complete shock, Yahweh is depicted as an out-of-her-mind grief-stricken mother careening through the mall on Christmas Eve, desperately screaming at the top of her lungs for a beloved child who has been lost: *"Where are you?"*

The Almighty Creator's response to our choice of going it alone on this third rock from the sun is a brokenhearted scream that rattles the universe with big-bang fury: *"Where are you?"* This scream, by the way, is echoed thousands of years later on an obscure hill called Golgotha by a second Adam whose tormented cry is, *"My God, My God, where are You?"*

Sort of changes things, doesn't it? Instead of a big, bad, boogeyman God who is so disappointed in you, one who can't wait for you to cross some imaginary moral line in the sand so you can be discarded like yesterday's garbage into the ash heap of hell, this passage portrays a grieving Parent who scours the landscape in search of lost children. What if all that fury, fire, and fearsomeness used to describe God in the Old Testament is really about God's love for us and not God's judgment of us? Crazy? The written record of Hebrew seers is spiced with ecstatic utterances from prophets and lovers intoxicated by this living, incomprehensible passion of the Divine Other.

> Can a mother forget the baby at her breast
> and have no compassion on the child she has borne?
> Though she may forget,
> I will not forget you!
> See, I have engraved you on the palms of my hands . . .
> (Isaiah 49:15–16 NIV)

> The Holy One your God is with you,
> Yahweh is mighty to save.
> Yahweh will take great delight in you,
> Yahweh will quiet you with love,
> Yahweh will rejoice over you with singing.
> (Zephaniah 3:17)

Contrast this with the response of the human beings. They hid. They hid from God, they hid from each other, and they hid from themselves. The sad reality is we are still hiding.

We hide.

God seeks.

A TRAVEL AGENT FOR GUILT TRIPS

Now the major side effect of this sin problem is it causes relational breakdown: we become more distant from others, from ourselves, and from God.

I bring all this up because I have observed that folks with relational problems generally have more pain at the end of life than those who don't. A lot more. There are exceptions of course, like patients who have a tumor pressing against a nerve. But by and large it is the people with large amount of existential relational pain that require more analgesics to find comfort as death approaches.

I've met many people like Jack who are acutely aware of their "problem." And, after more than thirty years of ministry, the only antidote to this relational problem I have discovered is forgiveness. In fact, I can't remember one troubled person I have counseled for whom forgiveness was not an issue. Not one. I'll go a step further and say I know of no more powerful or effective spiritual tool than forgiveness.

One of those enigmatic stories Jesus told, called parables, has to do with this very issue.

> Therefore, the kingdom of heaven is like a king who wanted to settle accounts with his servants. As he began the settlement, a man who owed him ten thousand talents was brought to him. Since he was not able to pay, the master ordered that he and his wife and his children and all that he had be sold to repay the debt.
>
> The servant fell on his knees before him. "Be patient with me," he begged, "and I will pay back everything." The servant's master took pity on him, canceled the debt and let him go.
>
> But when that servant went out, he found one of his fellow servants who owed him a hundred denarii. He grabbed him and began to choke him. "Pay back what you owe me!" he demanded.
>
> His fellow servant fell to his knees and begged him, "Be patient with me, and I will pay you back."

> But he refused. Instead, he went off and had the man thrown into prison until he could pay the debt. When the other servants saw what had happened, they were greatly distressed and went and told their master everything that had happened.
>
> Then the master called the servant in. "You wicked servant," he said, "I canceled all that debt of yours because you begged me to. Shouldn't you have had mercy on your fellow servant just as I had on you?" In anger his master turned him over to the jailers to be tortured, until he should pay back all he owed.
>
> This is how my heavenly Father will treat each of you unless you forgive your brother from your heart. (Matthew 18:23–35 NIV)

To really appreciate what Jesus was talking about here we need an understanding of the amounts of money referenced in the story. The tax the entire nation of Israel paid to Rome in one year added up to one thousand talents. So ten thousand talents would be the equivalent of ten years' worth of taxes—for the whole nation! By contrast, a hundred denarii is about two grand in our currency.

So here we have a servant who has squandered billions of dollars with nothing to show for it. Not the brightest bulb on the tree! And, as ridiculous as it might seem, he asks the king for more time to pay the debt back. How much time do you think the servant will need to save enough from his minimal wages to pay back billions of dollars? Laughable isn't it? The point is, this is a debt that could never be repaid. Yet the servant begs for more time, as if it will make a difference.

Note that the king does not grant the servant's request. The king does not give the servant "more time" to pay the debt back. In an incredible act of generosity, the king cancels the debt. Writes off billions with the stroke of a pen.

Now, you would think the servant would be jumping out of his skin with gratitude, joy, and excitement. Talk about hitting the lottery! Shockingly, as soon as he leaves the king's presence, he finds a guy who owes him about $2,000, throttles the guy, and demands the money he is owed. Now right about here, the story breaks down for most of us. How is the servant's behavior to be believed? Who could be so ungrateful?

I think the servant really had no way of comprehending what had just taken place in the king's presence. He was so stressed out about what he owed, so afraid about the torture that he, his wife, and his children might face, that he simply did not understand that his unrepayable debt had been forgiven. He asked for more time—but the king cancelled the debt. Yet, tragically, the servant doesn't understand what the king has done. He leaves the king's presence thinking he now has more time to pay back the debt and goes out looking for everyone owing him money—so he can pay the debt that has already been cancelled! It's crazy.

It's crazy, but I understand it.

A number of years ago, when I was still working as a travel agent for guilt trips, I was preaching on this text at my church. I was coming to the big wrap-up—the altar call. (You've probably seen it on TV: people come to the front of the church, crying, asking to be saved or forgiven or the like.) I could see the folks squirming in the pews.

"And you're just like this servant," I was bellowing, "God's forgiven you so much, a debt you could never repay, and still you hold grudges."

I was laying it on pretty thick when God started to speak to me. There I was, reminding this crowd of people how unforgiving they all were, when God interrupted me. Unfortunately, I can multitask, which means my mouth will sometimes continue working even when my brain is disengaged. (Just ask my wife!) So I continued preaching, even while having an inner dialogue with God.

God said, "You're the man."

"Whaddya mean by that?" I replied, hoping to hear God say what a fine instrument I was for bringing about conviction (which is the job of the Holy Spirit, by the way). But God had a different word for me.

"You're the guilty one. You're just like the servant in the story. I've forgiven all the hurtful things you've ever pulled, but still you are emotionally shaking down everyone in your life because you think they're the ones keeping you from being the perfect man you think I want."

Unbelievably, I just kept preaching, making those in attendance feel guilty while I continued my own dialogue with God.

"You're angry with your church," God continued, "because they're not bringing more people to hear you preach. Somehow, you think my love for you is based on how big the congregation is. And you're angry at your wife and your infant son because he isn't sleeping through the night, so you have to act like a father and help care for him, which means you have less time to pray and study the Bible. You believe your wife and your child are keeping you from being the holy man you think I want you to be. You act like you think I'm an ogre!"

With that, I finally and mercifully shut up. Busted.

Right there at the big altar call I humbly stood in front of my family and friends and confessed that I was the wicked servant. I was the one who desperately needed to hear the altar call that morning. I asked them to forgive me and pray for me.

The poor servant in Jesus' story simply didn't understand he had been forgiven. Neither did I.

Jesus concludes his story by saying that the servant was handed over to "the tormentors." That's what happens when we choose not to forgive—we are the ones who are tormented.

But often forgiveness just isn't that easy. It's loaded with emotion. It's not always rational. We cling to our wounds. There are times when I admit that I don't want to forgive. I'd rather stay hurt and fantasize about revenge. Sometimes I imagine the ones who have hurt me squirming as they realize their utter stupidity, begging for mercy but finding none. But as the old saying goes, unforgiveness is a poison we ingest hoping someone else will die. Unforgiveness shrivels the soul.

Forgiveness—like wisdom, compassion, and other life-enriching gifts—is not merely a matter of supernatural spiritual will power. It requires *grace*—and often that comes in its own good time. Henri Nouwen keenly observed, "Only as people who have accepted forgiveness can we find the inner freedom to give it."[16] And accepting forgiveness isn't as easy as you might think. It requires humility and honesty—two spiritual qualities often in short supply.

Modern-Day Dante

I do not think you should get rid of your sin
until you have learned what it has to teach you.

—Richard Rohr, *Falling Upward*

One of the luxuries of my time working for a small community hospital was that I was able to practice my chaplaincy in both hospital and hospice settings at the same time. They are different kinds of work. By and large, hospital patients have hope of recovering from illness and resuming their lives, albeit with some modifications. Not so with hospice patients. Hospice patients realize there is no recovery. So working in a small-town hospital afforded me the privilege of building relationships with people in the hospital, before they were facing a crisis.

I first met Billy when he was a patient at the hospital. He was affable, gravelly voiced, and full of stories. Most patients I meet in the hospital are not too eager to spend time with a chaplain. Not Billy. He seemed genuinely pleased to see me. As soon as I introduced myself he said, "Praise the Lord! I'm a Christian. I love Jesus with all of my heart! How about you?" During the visit, Billy told me his body was falling apart. His kidneys, his heart, his lungs—nothing was working right. So it was no surprise when I got the call a few weeks later and learned that Billy would be coming onto our hospice service.

When I arrived at Billy's house for our initial hospice visit, he was watching some television preacher on a religious channel. I noticed a large glass of red wine on the coffee table and a twelve-pack of beer next to Billy's chair. It was only four in the afternoon, but it smelled like Billy had been drinking for a while.

Billy turned off the televangelist and began to regale me with stories of being in Okinawa during World War II. He spoke of how relieved he was when we dropped "the big one" on Hiroshima and Nagasaki, since it meant he wouldn't be deployed to Japan in the effort to take the island by ground force. "Many lives were saved," he said over and over, justifying the use of atomic weaponry and minimizing his own fears of being deployed in a continued war effort.

He told me the cabin where he lived had once been a tavern—The Old Cedar Inn. It had been given to him years ago by the owner, Jimmy Swinehart, who explained to Billy, "I'm just paying taxes on it now anyway." The old abandoned tavern was falling in on itself, so Billy tore much of it down and rebuilt the remainder into his home. "The bar was over there where my bed is now," he said. Billy had lived in this makeshift cabin for more than fifty years.

Billy had three children, two of whom he didn't see very much. He told me, "All families have spats from time to time. Why can't everybody just get along?" Joyce, the one daughter Billy still spoke to, lived just a stone's throw from his cabin. I remember the day I met Joyce. She tearfully told me about her father's alcoholism and how he had abused her, her sisters, and her mother. When she was only eight years old, Joyce and her siblings had to sit outside the bar in the car on Saturday nights, sometimes until five in the morning, waiting for their dad to come out and begin the dreaded drunken drive home. Although her sisters wanted nothing to do with their father, she was still devoted to him, the only one willing to take care of him. She never married.

Once I got to know Billy, I learned that it was best to visit him in the morning. (Billy had an inviolate law that he wouldn't start drinking before noon, and I wanted to try and speak with the sober Billy.) One morning, with Bob the dog lying on the floor at his feet, Billy was retelling some of his favorite stories—old stories from his war days, stories from his early days here in Oregon, stories about all his old drinking buddies now dead. As I listened I noticed the yellow-crusted toenails on his swollen feet, which he kept elevated on a torn ottoman in a vain effort to limit the swelling. It was then that I thought of Dante and his *Divine Comedy,* which I'd been reading the night before.

I was enthralled by how Dante created his epic poem in an effort to explain his own reality—particularly, the pain and devastation caused by the conflict between the Guelphs and the Ghibellines (medieval Democrats and Republicans who fought with swords and muskets, not just words). I was thinking about how this inspired Italian poet from the fourteenth century had given his life to creating a meta-story, a myth, to make sense of his reality—and how this story had helped make sense of reality for many other wounded people down through the centuries. Now, here was this modern-day Dante trying to do the same thing. Billy was trying to create a story that would give meaning to his pains, his failed dreams, and his flawed humanity. Billy was desperate to make sense out of the chaos that was his life.

On a whim, I asked Billy what story he would most want his buddies to remember him by. "If I were sitting with all your drinking buddies and asked them to tell me a story about you, what would they tell me?"

Billy looked as if I'd slapped him in the face. He couldn't say anything. I pressed him, but he wouldn't give me an answer. He just sat silently, staring at the floor. Finally, after a long while, he said, "Chaplain, pray for me. . . . I've done some bad things." That was the closest he ever came to sharing his dark side with me. Billy just couldn't go there.

It's been suggested that we are formed by the stories we tell ourselves. That is to say, our behavior is deeply influenced by, or maybe even determined by, the narratives we use to give meaning to our experiences. If we want to change our behavior, we have to change the narrative we tell ourselves.

As I was driving down the mountain from Billy's house that day, I thought about the myths I have created to make sense of my own pain and flawed humanity. I wondered what stories my friends would tell to remember me? What stories do I tell myself that are currently shaping my behavior?

THE SHADOW KNOWS

In his work with the terminally ill, Canadian psychiatrist Harvey Chochinov observed that people's perceptions of themselves can have a profound influence on their experience of dying. Over the years he developed what he calls "dignity therapy" to help patients express their lives from their own conditioned perspective. In short, he simply encourages people to tell their own stories.

My own observation is that when dying people can tell their own stories with humility and honesty—sharing not just their joy and triumphs but also their shadow sides without excuses or shame—they are much more at peace with the whole process of dying. The reality is, the shadow is a part of each person's story.

Why do we run from our shadows? I once heard a fascinating lecture by Father Richard Rohr exploring this very subject. Drawing insights from the work of Carl Jung, Rohr suggested our dark sides (our demons) have much to teach us about ourselves. When we ignore and repress them, said Rohr, we actually stunt our spiritual growth. Thomas Moore, another Jungian disciple, goes even further: "The uniqueness of a person is made up of the insane and the twisted as much as it is of the rational and normal."[17] Now, Rohr and Moore are not suggesting we just give in and grab whatever forbidden fruit our flawed false selves desire in search of some momentary pleasure. But they are advising that we sit with our sins, contemplate them, and listen to what they are trying to tell us about our wounded humanity. In other words, we need to embrace our shadow selves, to make friends with them, and, in so doing, disarm them.

According to this insight, Billy's alcoholism was evidence of a parched soul aching to be quenched. What was Billy thirsty for? I don't know. And it's not important that I know the answer for Billy. The more pertinent question is, "What am I thirsty for?" What are my addictive, out-of-control behaviors trying to tell me? Rather than fear these flaws in my soul and hide from them, maybe I should listen to them?

When we refuse to face our fears, we actually empower them. I don't know if I learned this from reading Buddhists or from twelve-step meetings—but it's true. *What we resist persists.* The more energy we put into *not* talking about something unpleasant or *not* facing a difficulty in our lives, the more we feed that issue and give it power over us. This truth reveals some of the genius behind the Catholic sacrament of Reconciliation. In the sacrament, a person is encouraged to tell the truth—to face the reality of one's sin head on, without flinching, naming it and bringing it into the light of day with the aid of an accepting trusted advisor. There can be so much healing in simply stating the worst about ourselves to another person and receiving that person's loving acceptance in return. Many of the dying people I've been with have taught me that the really difficult issues become more manageable if we come out and talk about them. When we do this, those issues lose their power over us.

Unfortunately, in religious settings, talk about sin often causes feelings of shame and condemnation rather than the soul liberation that flows from the loving acceptance of God. As a result, all our fire-and-brimstone preaching has produced are overscrupulous nit-pickers. As one who has been on both sides of the pulpit, as a preacher and sinner, I have discovered that trying to please God by being good is a fool's game. We can never earn God's love by doing more good things than bad things. Spiritually speaking, "good enough" never is; instead, it is a ruthless taskmaster always demanding more. As the apostle Paul asserts in his exasperated cry from Romans, chapter 7:

> It happens so regularly that it's predictable. The moment I decide to do good, sin is there to trip me up. I truly delight in God's commands, but it's pretty obvious that not all of me joins in that delight. Parts of me covertly rebel, and just when I least expect it, they take charge.
>
> I've tried everything and nothing helps. I'm at the end of my rope. Is there no one who can do anything for me? Isn't that the real question? The answer, thank God, is that Jesus Christ can and does. (Romans 7:24–25 MSG)

Suffice it to say this deep awareness of our own sin, like grief, can either be a liberating awakening or a condemning experience that leads to greater isolation. What makes the difference? I suggest it is this *awful grace of God,* this grace wrapped in pain but with liberating power. My experience is when people are seized by this awful grace, they become reconciled to themselves, which enables them to be reconciled with others. This grace, this loving acceptance of God, frees us to rewrite the narratives that have enslaved us for years. Change, authentic change from the inside out, is now possible. A new internal script for living becomes available, one that is inclusive rather than exclusive, one that is compassionate rather than condemning.

Thomas Merton is one of my most trusted spiritual guides. Merton was a Catholic monk who spent more than twenty-five years living behind the walls of a monastery in Kentucky, trying to become holy. Near the end of his life, he gave up trying to be better than other people and wrote, "Thank God! Thank God! I am only another member of the human race, like all the rest of them. . . ."[18] Merton discovered that our flaws are what connect us to one another. It's like humanity is one big twelve-step group: "Hello, my name is Fred, and I'm a sinner." I belong.

When Billy would share about his faith, he often left me with the feeling he was trying to talk himself into believing it was all true—that at least he wasn't as bad as other people and, more importantly, that God really loved him. I wonder if the impetus compelling Billy to his frequent and loud verbal declarations of faith in Jesus was Billy's deep-seated hatred of himself—a self-loathing that gave evidence of Billy's estrangement from himself.

WHAT ARE YOU DOING HERE?

Like Billy, I spent many years in my own practice of Christianity attempting to earn God's love and acceptance. I know what it is to love God with all of your heart, yet hate yourself.

I was first seized by the love of Jesus when I was nineteen years of age. Before that time, I had no sexual experiences I can remember. Later that year, I woke up in the middle of a wet dream one night, and then realized what everyone had been talking about during my teenage years.

In no time at all, I became addicted to pornography. I know the feeling of an unseen force welling up from inside and compelling you to make choices against your heart's desire. I remember times, as a Spirit-filled believer, I would go to XXX-rated theaters in New York City. What I find so amazing is that, even there, grace came to me. As I sat in the darkness of those theaters, overwhelmed by fear and shame, the Beloved's voice would come to me: *"What are you doing here? What are you doing here?"* The words were not spoken in condemnation but in compassion. Not in rejection but in acceptance.

I know the feeling of leaving places like that, terrified you'll run into someone you know. I know what it is to love God with all your heart and hate yourself. But I also know what it is to be forgiven and liberated by grace.

Psychologist Thomas Moore writes:

> A soulful life is never without shadow, and some of the soul's power comes from its shadow qualities. If we want to live from our depths—soulfully—then we will have to give up all pretenses to innocence as the shadow grows darker. The chief reward of surrendering innocence, so that the soul may be fully expressed, is an increase of power. In the presence of deep power, life becomes robust and passionate, signs that the soul is engaged and being given expression.[19]

According to Moore, embracing the shadow helps life become "robust and passionate." One of the ways we achieve this is by embracing our dark sides and sharing them with others. This honest self-disclosure helps create space for deeper relationships with others, for community. As we slay the giant of self-hatred, we also till the hardened soil of our souls and become fertile for truly loving relationships.

Which Way Home?

■

Come, come, whoever you are.

Wanderer, worshiper, lover, or drunk

It doesn't matter.

Ours is not a caravan of despair.

Come even if you have broken your vows a hundred times.

Come, come again to hope.

—Rumi

This acceptance stuff is a big deal. We all are driven by it—some to extremes. For example, I remember a hospice patient named Darla. She told me that every weekend, she and her husband travel 165 miles each way to go to church. They belong to a small, strict Christian sect. They drive up on Saturday night so they can be there for early "instruction" (training to become a full member) before the regular worship service on Sunday mornings. They stay for Bible study in the afternoon, then Sunday evening service, and spend the night before returning home on Monday morning. According to Darla, they do all this because they "want to be saved." "Saved" is a religious code word for being accepted by God. Darla shared, "My biggest fear is not being in God's will." More than five hundred years after Martin Luther, we're still struggling with the old works-versus-grace argument.

I was thinking about Darla one morning as I read a passage from Karl Rahner that spoke about "the totality of humanity which God will never allow to escape from his love."[20] I was struck by the absolute incongruity of these two worldviews. I can easily identify with where my friend Darla is coming from. For so much of my Christian life I was terrified—terrified of missing it, of going to hell, of not being saved, of not being acceptable to God. I lived my life in fear. That's why I'd argue so vigorously with anyone who disagreed with me. If they were right, I might be wrong. And being wrong meant going to hell.

Then there are people like Rahner, gifts from God who understand that God already accepts us. They remind the rest of us that God "will not allow us to escape God's love for us." This is a truth so powerful it can actually create the conditions for spiritual liberty, a truth that leads naturally to living freely. Now, I'm not suggesting that God ignores the selfish choices (sin) we make. My point is that our choice about whether we root ourselves in grace or in works will drastically affect how we live. It will determine whether our lives are characterized by fear or freedom. I want to be in Rahner's camp, but the truth is, on any given day and depending on my personal behavior, I'm in the works camp. I switch camps pretty regularly.

IT'S ALL GREEK TO ME

There are a couple of ancient Greek stories that help clarify the point I'm trying to make, and they both involve the Sirens. According to Greek myth, the Sirens were cannibals who could disguise themselves as beautiful women with a magical ability to sing. They lived on an island, and whenever a boat of men came passing by, they would run down to the seashore, disguise themselves as women, and sing their enchanting songs. The men in the boat would hear the music of the Sirens, lose all sense of sanity, draw near to the shore, crash upon the rocks hidden under the surf, and be devoured by the cannibals.

Ulysses and his men had to pass by the island of the Sirens to get home from the Trojan War, but Ulysses was smarter than your average bear. He'd heard about the Sirens and took precautions. He melted wax and put it in the ears of his crew so they wouldn't be distracted by the Sirens' song and follow it to their destruction. But he wanted to hear their enchanted music, so he did not plug his own ears. Instead, he had his men lash him to the mast of the boat and told them, "As we go by the island, don't listen to anything I say—just keep rowing. Don't look left or right, just row."

When Ulysses's boat went by the island, the Sirens came down to the shore disguised as beautiful women and sang their song. Ulysses's men couldn't hear a thing. But Ulysses almost went crazy. He was so enchanted by the music that he was writhing against the ropes that bound him and screaming at his men, "Men, stop! Stop the boat! Don't you understand? We're home! These are our wives! Stop!" Fortunately, his men couldn't hear a thing.

This is a wonderful word picture of how I long sought to live my Christian life. While working hard to pilot my ship to heaven, I was always being tempted to veer off course into one sin or another (the Sirens' song)—but I was terrified of offending God and going to hell. I nearly drove myself and everyone around me crazy.

There is another way.

Like Ulysses, Jason, the captain of the ship *Argo*, had to go by the island of the Sirens in his search for the Golden Fleece. But

Jason had another plan. Jason brought along a magical flute player. As Jason's ship went by the Sirens' island, the crew heard the enchanted singing and began directing the ship toward the shore. But Jason simply cued the magic flute player. When the men in the ship heard the extraordinary beauty of the flute music, the Sirens' song was no longer enticing but instead sounded discordant and off key. It lost its power. Jason's men were no longer tempted to destruction when they heard a more beautiful song.

Hearing the beautiful song of God's loving acceptance of us is an experience of grace, a melody that is much more captivating than the many other songs that seduce us to danger. Listening to God's grace helps us stay on course to get safely home.[21]

The prophet Zephaniah calls out to us from across the centuries to tell us the Beloved will "quiet us in love" and "rejoice over us with singing" (Zephaniah 3:15 NIV). Can you imagine it? God sings over you and me with rejoicing. We bring pleasure to God.

THE SONG OF GOD

I still vividly remember the day I heard that more beautiful song.

A number of years before I started my training to become a chaplain my wife and I were living in Windsor, England (home of the famous castle). I was a traveling preacher then and part of the leadership team of a small network of churches. We'd been living in England for a little more than a year, but we'd already had to move three times. The last place we landed was a two-story dwelling on Washington Close in Windsor. As I remember, it was a very grey house. The exterior trim was painted white to offset the large, brownish grey stone construction. It had a small manageable yard (or a "garden," as the English like to say). The whole neighborhood was built on the ancient dump site for the castle. So while we lived on a small hill, the ground (and, therefore, the foundation of the house) was shifting. None of the doors in the house would close without effort. Everything seemed just a little off kilter—and not just with the house itself.

As I say, it just felt grey. That was probably due in no small measure to the fact that it was at this house on Washington Close that my beloved Cyndi entered a two-year deep, deep depression.

I felt so inept. Here was the woman I loved—my wife, my partner of twelve years—in intense pain, and I couldn't do a damn thing to make it better. We prayed. Oh, God, how we prayed for relief. We cried. Cyndi went for counseling. We cried some more. My own self-doubt and sense of failure were debilitating. Was I responsible for her depression? What kind of husband was I? What kind of Christian minister was I?

To help alleviate my own pain, I began riding a stationary bike. I was obsessive about it—an hour every day. I would sit atop that bike in a tiny upstairs spare bedroom, blankly staring out the window onto the deserted grey cul-de-sac, and ride like a man possessed. This went on for months. I fell out of favor (not blamelessly) with the church network. We were foreigners, all alone in a strange land. That bike was my only place of refuge.

I remember I'd been invited to speak at a gathering of church leaders during a missions conference. I had nothing to say. I was afraid, overwhelmed, angry, and alone. The Friday before the conference, I attempted to pray in the hope of coming up with something intelligent to share at the meeting.

Nothing. God was silent. I was angry, and God was silent—which only made me more angry. Eventually, my default mechanism kicked in, and I got on my bike. I began pedaling, thinking to myself, "What am I going to do? I have nothing to say."

As I continued to ride, I remembered a creative exercise I once heard about to help you connect with God. The goal was to close your eyes and imagine Judgment Day. Imagine the Great White Throne, the sea of glass, the four and twenty elders. Everyone who has ever lived is gathered together in a great hall for final judgment. It's a massive sea of people that stretches beyond eyesight. One by one, each person's name is called out, and the great crowd of humanity parts to allow the person called to step forward and approach Almighty God. Each individual stands before God, all alone, and looks God right in the eye—eyeball to eyeball with God.

The first time I did this what I imagined was God turning away in disgust—like I was a big disappointment. That freaked me out so I tried a second time. This time when I looked into God's face I saw God had kind of a Mona Lisa smile. I didn't know if God was amused or upset with me. I just couldn't tell. That wasn't much better so I tried again.

What I saw the third time changed my life. This time, when God saw me, tears of joy began to stream down the Beloved's cheeks. God laughed a loud, hearty laugh. Then the Beloved grabbed Jesus and they began to sing and dance: "He's home! Our son made it! Our plan worked. He's home!" With this revelation, I began to cry very hard. I felt waves of God's love and acceptance come over me. It was as if all my feelings of shame and failure had melted away. It was no longer important to me where I was or how I made my living. I had the experience of feeling God loves me just like I am—despite my screw-ups.

The whole experience took me by surprise. I was not expecting God to reveal Godself to me as I sat pedaling my exercise bike like a hamster on a wheel. But in that moment, grace was no longer simply a word but an overwhelming experience.

I was surprised to feel that God actually had fun during this whole game watching me learn.

I was surprised too at my own need to justify myself before God. I had preached in many places about how we can never earn God's love, but I realized that was exactly what I'd been trying to do. I was unable to accept unmerited favor—grace—for myself.

What if God really loves all of us just as we are—imperfections, incorrect theology, and all?

What if our discovery of God brings God joy?

What could we become if we allowed God's love and acceptance—God's grace—to overwhelm us?

David and Goliath

■

If you discover that somebody really loves you, listens to you, then you begin to change. You come out from behind the barriers of fear that you have erected around your heart.

—Jean Vanier, *Encountering "the Other"*

I MET DAVID early in my chaplaincy career while working at a hospice house in Missouri. It was a beautiful center that looked and felt more like a spa than a medical facility, yet it was a place where people came to die. David was Jewish, loved music, and had been married four times. (He loved women, too.) His only child was an adopted daughter who was my age, mid-fifties, and lived five hours away. He told me the best gift he'd ever given his wives was to divorce them. He confided dryly, "I wasn't a good husband." David was dying of COPD—chronic obstructive pulmonary disease (bad lungs). For nearly four months, I visited David twice a week, and we became very close.

David and I both enjoyed verbal sparring. Like me, he was an armchair philosopher who loved to argue. Sometimes we would even switch sides of an issue in the same conversation. We were two peas in a pod.

At one point during David's stay at the hospice house, the director wanted to discharge him. To put it bluntly, David was a pain in the ass. He'd taken it as his personal mission to change the entire food service program at the house. Traditionally, meals came at 8 A.M., noon, and 5 P.M., which meant residents couldn't get anything to eat from 5:30 P.M. until 8 the next morning. And they had no choice about the menu; they got whatever was prepared. David would call the kitchen up to five times a day with suggestions, and would also e-mail the house administrators numerous times each day.

Meanwhile, several months prior to David's arrival, the director of the house had been negotiating a contract with the hospital next door that would allow for a new menu with three choices for each meal, every day, and no repetition of meals for at least a month. In addition, the meals could be ordered by patients any time between 6 A.M. and 9 P.M. When this program was finally about to launch, the house director wanted to make sure everyone—staff and residents alike—knew the new menu was her idea and had nothing to do with David's barrage of phone calls and e-mails. At IDG (a weekly interdisciplinary group meeting) I objected. I told the hospice house team I believed that working for these menu changes had become a source of meaning for David as he neared death. Advocating for a meal plan that would better meet the needs of the residents was David's reason for living. If we let him believe he'd been responsible for these changes, he might actually find some peace and let go. The medical director of the hospice house agreed with my assessment.

Graciously, the house director agreed to thank David for all his hard work and credited him for the new menu changes. David confided to me that he was so pleased to leave behind a legacy "for everyone that will come here after me." In David's Jewish tradition, being remembered after death was very important. David felt he had fulfilled this possibility for himself and that helped him achieve a measure of peace.

But as David was approaching death, he left word at the nurse's station that he did not want his daughter notified when he was actively dying. This request had all the hospice house nurses in an uproar. David's case manager ordered me to talk to David about this, because she thought this request was totally unfair. (And, yes, I did mention to the case manager that this was her issue, not his.) But I didn't have to bring it up in my next meeting with David, because he asked about it straightaway as soon as I walked into his room. For nearly half an hour, David loudly defended his right to be alone when he died. I let him vent. Finally, after all the air was out, I asked him why he was treating his adult daughter like a child by not letting her decide if she wanted to be with him while he was dying. He shot right back at me, "Okay, do you want to know the truth? The truth is I'm afraid she won't want to be here! Okay?"

"Fair enough," I replied, "that's the first honest thing I've heard you say about it—and I support your decision." I understood right there and then that the Goliath in David's life was the same giant I'd long been battling: the fear of rejection. David and I both dealt with that fear in the same way, by pushing people away before they could reject us.

On my next visit, David asked me if it would be all right for the nurses to contact me when he was dying, so I could come be with him. I teasingly said, "I thought you didn't want anyone to be with you. You wanted to die alone." David gruffly said, "I have the right to change my mind, don't I? Besides, you're my chaplain!" I was deeply touched and joyfully agreed to his request.

The next weekend David's daughter came for a monthly visit, and they had a very tender time of reconciliation. As they lay on his bed watching a movie, David asked his daughter if she would come be with him when he was dying. With tears she said, "Of course." And that's how David slew Goliath.

I'll never forget my last meeting with David. It was my last day at the hospice house. I'd accepted another chaplaincy position halfway across the country, and David was hoping he would die before I left. Truth be told, I was too. During my last week there, some staff members found David walking (with his walker) as fast as he could down the hallway late at night. He told me later he was trying to make himself have a heart attack. On my last Friday afternoon, after I'd lingered with him for some time, he just tearfully said, "Please just go. I won't turn around to say goodbye . . . I love you." With that, we hugged—and I left.

On Monday morning at around 8:30, just as I getting ready to begin the two-thousand-mile drive to my new job, a staff member from the hospice house called to tell me David had died an hour ago. So I made a short detour before setting off; I went to the house to see David. His body was lying on his bed. I sat in the chair next to him and just cried. I missed my friend. After about half an hour, I looked at his dead body and without thinking said to his spirit, "Come on, are you up for a road trip? Let's go to Oregon." So, for the next four days, I sensed David with me in the car as I drove west. We argued the whole way.

Death of a Do-Gooder

I will never be able to find myself if I isolate myself from the rest of mankind as if I were a different kind of being.

—Thomas Merton, *New Seeds of Contemplation*

As I mentioned earlier, my wife and I, along with our son, Elijah, spent several years living abroad in England, where I was part of the leadership team for a small network of churches. For a variety of reasons, things didn't go well, so we moved back to Florida. This was one of the lowest points in my life. I felt like such a failure; I felt shamed. After a lot of soul searching, I decided one way I might get some fresh air from my depression was by helping someone else. As a way of honoring the memory of my friend Petey, I became a volunteer at a local house for persons with AIDS.

As you might imagine, when I showed up announcing that I was an evangelical preacher who "just wanted to help out," I was viewed with some skepticism. Many folks whose theological beliefs are similar to mine have inflicted serious wounds on persons living with AIDS; honestly, that's one of the reasons I wanted to be there. I don't think Jesus would treat people with AIDS the way many who claim to follow him do. As I read the Gospels, Jesus seemed to welcome those considered untouchable in his culture, and they were attracted to him—not repelled and put off by him.

For about a year, I went down to the AIDS house every Wednesday to have lunch with some of the folks there and get to know them. I had no hidden agenda. I just wanted to express my belief that God loves us all very much—regardless of whom we may or may not have slept with.

Truth be told, when I first showed up, I was scared shitless. I had no idea what I was doing. I had no training to be with dying people (this was shortly before my studies began to become a chaplain), nor had I spent much time with people who were openly gay, as were most of the men living here. Add in my emotional hard wiring as an introvert, and this situation had all the makings of another disaster. Maybe it was the pungent aroma of my fear, but three guys in particular made space for me in their hearts and at their lunch table—Billy, Elliot, and John.

Over the course of that year, I spent lunch every Wednesday with these three guys, cracking jokes, talking about the Yankees or the news, and telling stories about my dog McDuff, or about how my teenage son was pushing my buttons. They were pretty much housebound due to their disease, so they seemed to love to hear stories about the outside world, stories about what a "normal" family life is like. Then, after lunch, we'd play pool.

The highlight of the year came on my birthday, when they decided they wanted to take me to a gay bar around the corner from the AIDS house. Needless to say, I had never, ever, been to a gay bar. But I sensed that my accepting their "gift" was a test of our growing friendship, so I agreed to go. I don't know if I've ever felt more out of place. Mercifully, the bar had a pool table, so I was able to hide out playing pool with Billy for most of the time there. Elliot and John had a great time flirting with the bartender, and they bragged for weeks about how another patron had bought them both drinks.

I drank a couple of beers while playing pool with Billy, which meant, eventually, that I needed to use the bathroom. Frankly, the idea of going into the bathroom at a gay bar terrified me. I don't know what I thought might happen in there—maybe I'd walk in on some guys "doing it" in a stall, or maybe I was afraid someone would think I was going in there to look for some "action"—but there was no way in hell I was going into the bathroom! I had vivid images of my bladder bursting and my entrails exploding all over the pool table, but I managed to hold out until we finally left. After I dropped the guys off at the house, I sped to the McDonald's just down the street, ran to the urinal, and peed like a racehorse.

The next Wednesday the guys asked about my apparent aversion to the bathroom at the bar. They'd noticed that I'd had a few beers but never went to relieve myself—and they teased me ruthlessly. We laughed for months afterward about our big night out at the bar.

Later that year, John had a stroke, which left him in a wheelchair. Because he was no longer ambulatory, Florida state law required that John leave the home for a full-care facility (a nursing home). If there had been a fire at the AIDS house, he wouldn't have been able to escape by himself—hence the move.

So my weekly routine was now to go down to the AIDS house for lunch and a game of pool with Billy (who had a slight learning disability), and then Elliot, Billy, and I would pile into my pick-up truck and head over to the nursing home to see John. On the way to the nursing home, we would always stop by Wendy's to pick up four small Frostys. Frostys were the highlight of the week.

One day as we were heading to the nursing home with Frostys in hand, Billy wanted to ask me a question. I said, "Sure . . . what's up?"

"Why won't my penis get hard anymore?" he wanted to know.

How did I get here? I imagined what the friends from my previous church would think if they could see me now. Most would think I was some kind of heretic. I simply told Billy, "I don't answer penis questions. You'd better ask Elliot."

Elliot told Billy he should ask his doctor, and suggested Billy get a testosterone supplement.

I realized I was way out of my element.

Later, as we were pulling up at the nursing home to visit John, a life-changing event occurred. As we were getting out of the pickup, a car pulled up behind us, and a woman I'd never seen before got out. She asked if we were the guys from the AIDS house. We froze. Time seemed to stand still. Everything within me wanted to scream, "Wait a minute. I'm just a volunteer. I drive the truck and buy the Frostys—that's all. I'm not a homosexual and I do not have AIDS!" But I saw my friends standing there and imagined how they'd feel. I didn't know who this woman was or what she wanted. But it was a defining moment in my life. I sensed the Spirit of Jesus come upon me, and I simply said, "Yeah, we're from the AIDS house."

I said this knowing full well she would assume I was gay and had AIDS. As I said, "Yeah," I felt something deep within my bowels break. I could almost hear it. I started to cry. I realized in that moment what it meant to identify with someone else, and the meaning of the word *compassion* traveled the eighteen inches from my head into my heart. A religious do-gooder died that afternoon as the compassion of God was born in me.

As it turned out, the woman was a social worker at the nursing home and simply wanted to let us know where we could find our friend John.

Driving home, I mulled over the story of Jesus being baptized in the Jordan River. Jesus was sinless. He didn't need to repent of anything or be baptized. But Jesus submitted to John's baptism in order to identify with the rest of us who need it. As Augustine so aptly put it, "God had one son on earth without sin, but never one without suffering." That's compassion.

The next week when I went back to the AIDS house, Elliot interrupted our normal routine. He didn't want me to go play pool with Billy. He didn't want to visit John. He didn't even want to get Frostys. He wanted to talk. Now, in the whole year I had been going to the AIDS house, I'd never had a serious discussion about spiritual things with anyone there—ever. Everyone knew I was a preacher, but we never discussed religion. However, one week after my breakthrough regarding real compassion, Elliot wanted to share with me some of his deepest fears.

He told me he had recurring nightmares about going to hell. It terrified him. I listened, not as a preacher but as a friend. I told him I'm not afraid of hellfire because I've come to believe God loves me just as I am—neurotic, selfish, immature, and overweight.

We both cried. Elliot told me that, in his fifty years of living, no one had ever told him God loved him. He'd always thought he wasn't good enough for God's love. After we talked for more than an hour, Elliot walked me to the truck, gave me a big hug, and told me that was the best conversation he'd had in more than ten years. It was the first time we'd ever hugged.

I am so grateful for my friends—Billy, John, and Elliot. They accepted me, loved me, and taught me about real compassion. They helped deliver me from being merely a religious do-gooder and enabled me to move toward becoming the kind of Christian I've always wanted to be.

It's Crying Time Again

Nobody escapes being wounded. We are all wounded people, whether physically, emotionally, mentally, or spiritually. The main question is not "How can we hide our wounds?" so we don't have to be embarrassed but "How can we put our woundedness in the service of others?" When our wounds cease to be a source of shame, and become a source of healing, we have become wounded healers.

—Henri Nouwen, *The Wounded Healer*

When a nurse calls for the chaplain because there is a patient or family member crying, the issue often has more to do with the nurse's discomfort at seeing pain she can't fix than the crying person's real need for spiritual care. But as a chaplain, you always come when called, to see if you can help.

So on Friday morning, when the charge nurse called and asked for my help with a crying family member, I went immediately.

Chandra was a Hindu woman in her thirties. In between her sobs, she told me that her father, Prakash, was in need of a liver transplant due to damage from hepatitis. But he was not a candidate for the transplant, because he had such a weak heart. As a result, Chandra's father was in our ICU, intubated (which means a plastic tube connected to a ventilator was inserted down his throat to help him breathe) and sedated (so he would not try to yank the aforementioned plastic tube out of his throat).

After calming down a little, Chandra took me to meet the rest of her family, who were camped out in the ICU waiting room. Her mother, Sachi, was a very short woman with a strong, quiet dignity. Her brother, Gadin, was tall and lean, and had just arrived from his home in Virginia. All were very concerned about the state of Prakash's health and knew death was a real possibility.

As I often do on a first encounter with family, I simply tried to make nice and be helpful. I showed them where the blankets and pillows were kept for family members. I informed them about the hours of our cafeteria's operation (without commenting about the quality of the food served there). And I told them that our Catholic hospital had a large beautiful chapel that was often empty, making it a great place to get away from the sights and sounds of the hospital.

They were very grateful for my welcome. As I gave them an extra box of tissues before leaving, I asked them to have me paged if there was anything more I could do.

The following Tuesday morning as I was making my rounds, I ran into Chandra again. She told me her father's health had improved and the plastic tube in his throat had been removed. He was out of the ICU and on the main floor, and he wanted to meet me.

As I entered his room, I noticed the NPO sign on Prakash's door. *NPO* is hospital code that means the patient is not allowed any food, or anything by mouth. Prakash had stark white hair and looked to be a tall man. The white sheets were tucked up tightly under his dark-skinned chin. I remember him as having a very kind face.

"Hi there, my name is Fred. I'm the chaplain for this floor, and I have had the privilege to meet your family. I've seen you a few times but you were asleep. It is very good to see you awake."

Chandra was seated next to her father's bed. "This is the man who gave me such confidence when you were in the ICU," she told him, then said something else to him in Hindi.

Very weakly, Prakash said, "Thank you for coming . . ."

"You look so much more beautiful without the tubes covering your face," I said teasingly.

"Thank you. I am a man who fears God. There is one God . . . for us all. My name is Prakash; it means 'light.'" Prakash then very kindly gave me a short tutorial on Hinduism, which I knew nothing about. He concluded by saying, "There are many paths but one destination. The rain falls and makes different streams that all go to the one sea."

After a long pause, I asked what he did when he wasn't occupying one of our hospital beds. He said he was a mathematician. "Oh, you must have a great brain," I offered.

With a huge smile he countered, "You're impressed with my brain, my doctor worries about my heart, now all I really need is a liver!" We all laughed.

Since Prakash was feeling short of breath and his lips had become dry, we concluded our conversation.

Before leaving, I asked Chandra if she could teach me a short Hindu prayer to pray for her father. She replied, "Om Shanti, Shanti—it means 'bring peace to the world.'"

That night, Prakash's condition drastically deteriorated—and so did my own. That evening, my son, Elijah, and I had another horrible war of words. In recent years, he and I had been growing apart. During his early teens, Elijah started making some life choices that caused quite a lot of pain for Cyndi and me. The details aren't important, but the pain was significant and intense. There were many fights and a lot of yelling and screaming, but little or no communication. It was another dark period of our family life. Coming home to yet another battle with him left me in a foul mood. There was no peace in my world.

By the time I returned to the hospital the next morning, Prakash was intubated, sedated, and back in the ICU. When I found his family in the waiting room—which had become the family's headquarters—Gadin was on his cell phone speaking to a cousin in Los Angeles who is a cardiologist, trying to confirm the information our doctors had given them about Prakash's condition.

As soon as Chandra saw me, she started to cry. "Where is the church in this hospital?" she blurted out.

I began to explain again about the Catholic chapel, but she cut me off: "Take me there now."

As we were walking down the hall to the chapel, Chandra was weeping uncontrollably and muttering, "I'm so afraid . . . I don't want to lose my papa. He told me to take care of my mother. He thinks he is dying . . . I can't lose him."

We entered the chapel and sat down near the front, to the right side of the altar. I handed Chandra a box of tissues, and we sat together in silence for a long time.

She began to pray from a Hindu prayer book she had with her, mixing chanting with prayers, but then she suddenly stopped and began to scream, "You're a cheater, God! You're a cheater, God! I want my papa. I want my papa."

At the front of the chapel was a large stone crucifix, about twenty feet tall. From where we were seated, the face of Jesus was turned away from us in agony.

"He won't even look at me! He's a cheater God. Look at me! Look at me!" she screamed at the crucifix. "I want my papa." She said the same thing over and over for a long time before she finally looked at me and very quietly said, "If he dies, I'll never pray again. I'll never go to Krishna's temple. I'll tear this up (she held up her Hindu prayer booklet), and I'll never pray again. . . . I vow that if he dies I will never pray again!"

There was a long silence. I said nothing. I was frozen. I had so many thoughts and emotions running through me. I considered how I would have responded to this situation just a few years prior. I probably would have tried to convert this Hindu woman to Christianity by proclaiming how our God is the true God and He would never let her down. Perhaps I would have tried to defend God by saying something like, "You just need to trust He's really here, even though you don't feel like He's here now." But at that moment, Chandra's raw grief uncorked some of my own anger issues with God about my son and our painful relationship. I wanted to say, "Move over, sister, and let me take a couple of whacks at Him. I've got my own issues!"

We sat there and cried together for a long time. She wept for a father, I, for a son. Both of us for our own pain.

Simply being in the presence of that kind of raw, deep grief is emotionally exhausting. It can also be very bonding.

The Spanish philosopher Miguel de Unamuno coined the term *amor spiritualis* ("spiritual love") to describe our relationships with others that makes us each more whole—more fully human. He writes:

> Spiritual love is born of sorrow. . . . For [people] love one another with a spiritual love only when they have suffered the same sorrow together, when through long days they have ploughed the stony ground buried beneath the common yoke of a common grief. It is then that they know one another and feel one another and feel with one another in their common

> anguish, and so thus they have pity [compassion] for one another and love one another. For to love is to have compassion; and if bodies are united by pleasure, souls are united by pain. . . . To love with the spirit is to have pity, and he [or she] who has compassion most loves most.[22]

De Unamuno has wisely observed that a uniquely profound bond can be forged when we share our woundedness with each other. My truest friends are the ones I have cried with. I can't speak for Chandra, but I know that sitting in the chapel for such a long time and crying together with her opened my heart to her and her family in a very deep way.

That evening I sat with Chandra's family in the Quiet Room as Prakash's doctor explained the dire prognosis for this man they all loved. Then he asked them a question no family wants to hear: "Do you still want us to do everything possible?"

Chandra, of course, was crying. Gadin sat staring blankly at the floor, his head in his hands. Sachi was stone silent. No one said a word.

"Maybe it will help to put the question differently," I offered. "Right now, it feels like you are being asked to decide if Prakash lives or dies." They all nodded. "But there is another way to look at it. The reality is we who work here at the hospital don't know Prakash. I had only one brief conversation with him, so I really never got to know him. You do. You've known him your whole lives. Instead of feeling like you're making this decision for him, you're really his voice now that he can't speak to us. If Prakash were sitting here, hearing everything the doctor just said and analyzing the situation, what would he tell us to do?"

After a long pause, Sachi spoke: "He would never want this. He would not want to be kept like this." Her children agreed. The doctor and I silently left to give the family time and space.

An hour later, they decided to turn off the ventilator. Later that night, Prakash died.

I saw Chandra and her family one final time the next morning as they were leaving the hospital. She actually looked much brighter than I'd ever seen her before. She wasn't crying. I noticed she was reading from her Hindu prayer booklet. She had gotten me a small gift to thank me for my service to her and her family. It was a candle. She told me that as the candle burned, the wax would melt into the shape of a butterfly.

I acknowledged how appropriate it was to have a candle to remember the man whose name meant "light." She smiled.

Noises Off

The final mystery is oneself.

—Oscar Wilde, "De Profundis"

THE DAY MARIO DIED was very noisy.

The nurse had called to tell me that Mario was actively dying and his caregivers had asked if I would come. I'd been visiting Mario once or twice a month for nearly a year, and in all that time I'd never heard him talk. He was a short man with a long European nose and waxy skin, and his glassy eyes always had a faraway look, as though he were somewhere else. On several of my visits, when I arrived and introduced myself (which I always did), he extended his hand for me to shake. That was the only response I ever got from Mario to indicate that he even knew I was present.

His caregivers told me that Mario was Roman Catholic and that his only family was a nephew who visited Mario weekly. The nephew had informed the caregivers Mario had already received the church's last rites from a priest.

Mario was living his final days in an adult foster home. (In Oregon, these homes allow four or five elderly patients to receive personal care when they can no longer live alone.) When I arrived at the home, Mario was lying in his bed staring out the window on his left, with that familiar faraway look. He was snoring loudly, yet his glassy eyes remained wide open.

I pulled a rocking chair close to Mario's bed so I could silently pray for him. But after I got settled in, it struck me how bizarre the whole scene was. I guess Mario liked Perry Como music, because the caregivers had a Perry Como CD playing on a boom box next to Mario's bed. As I sat down, Perry was belting out, "Hot-diggity, dog diggity, boom what you do to me . . ."

I began looking around Mario's room for clues to this little man with the faraway look. The first thing I noticed was a huge picture of John Wayne. It was an oil painting on black velvet. On the bureau was a framed photo of a young man in a military uniform, circa World War II. The man in the photo (I assume it was Mario) reminded me of Radar O'Reilly from TV's M★A★S★H. He looked so full of hope, so full of promise. On the wall above Mario's bed was a small, cheap, plastic crucifix. When I saw this, I started tripping out. I began to imagine some crummy factory in some poor nation where barefooted children were being paid a pittance to glue little plastic Jesuses on little plastic crosses so they could be sold for a big markup in religious stores in the United States. I asked myself, "Is this really what Jesus came and died for? Plastic Jesuses on little plastic crosses? My God, how we have so trivialized the Good News."

My (self-) righteous indignation had kicked into third gear when I was summoned back to the present moment by the screams of a demented woman in the next room. She was watching some cop show on TV and was yelling at the TV for Clark to get a million dollars to ransom her or else kidnappers were going to kill her!

"Hot-diggity, dog-diggity, boom what you do to me."

As I sat there amid the chaos and noise, trying to pray for Mario, looking at his vacant stare and the waxy shell that was his declining body, I remembered a thread from the morning's online chaplain chat room. Someone had raised the question, "When does the soul leave the body?" The thread had created quite a stir. It seems people (particularly ministers) have strong opinions about the afterlife and what happens to the soul. Looking at Mario, I wondered, was he in there? I mean, was that animated spark that made Mario uniquely Mario, his soul, still inside his body or had it already left? Did it leave long ago, hence the vacant far-off stare?

"Hot-diggity, dog-diggity, boom what you do to me."

THE WILD ANIMAL IN ME

Why do we fill our lives with so much noise? Cell phones, iPods, video games, TV—it's like we're terrified of being alone with ourselves for even a minute. Are we just killing time—or are we also killing our souls?

What is the soul anyway? So many people talk about the soul and just assume we all understand what is meant by the word. Is it that animated spark of the Divine so many people believe we all have? Is it the *imago Dei?* Are the words "soul" and "spirit" interchangeable? When does the soul leave the body? What happens to it after it leaves the body? These are the kinds of questions you ask if you want to start a fight. But when you're a chaplain and someone is dying and the family wants to know the answers and you're supposed to know the answers—it can all be kind of daunting.

As I have sat with dying persons like Mario, they have given me the space to explore these questions head on and have graciously allowed me to admit the terrifying truth that no one really knows for sure. Oh, I know, many of us have strong opinions about the answers to these questions—opinions taught to us by forceful preachers or inspiring writers or our own out-of-the-body experiences. But the bottom line is none of us really knows for sure. I have had to admit that I am being asked to provide a road map to a place to which none of us has ever been. The dying have reminded me that I must hold very lightly to my own strong opinions about these questions and humbly acknowledge I might be wrong.

St. Louis University professor Belden Lane was caring for his dying mother in a nursing home when he so honestly admitted, "All theologizing, if worth its salt, must submit to the test of hospital gowns, droning television sets, and food spilled in the clumsy effort to eat. What can be said of God that may be spoken without shame in the presence of those who are dying?"[23]

As important as these questions about the nature and destiny of the soul are, the more pertinent question for me right now is: How do I get in touch with my own soul? How do I excavate the dirt and rock of my own narcissistic false self and discover the gold of my true being that lies beneath? If we are all estranged from ourselves, how do we get unestranged?

Of all the descriptions of the soul I have encountered, none is as captivating to me as that put forward by the Quaker Parker Palmer, who compares the soul to a wild animal.

> Like a wild animal, the soul is tough, resilient, resourceful, savvy, and self-sufficient: it knows how to survive in hard places. I learned about these qualities during my bouts with depression. In that deadly darkness, the faculties I had always depended on collapsed. My intellect was useless; my emotions were dead; my will was impotent; my ego was shattered. But from time to time, deep in the thickets of my inner wilderness, I could sense the presence of something that knew how to

> stay alive even when the rest of me wanted to die. That something was my tough and tenacious soul.
>
> Yet despite its toughness, the soul is also shy. Just like a wild animal, it seeks safety in the dense underbrush, especially when other people are around. If we want to see a wild animal, we know that the last thing we should do is go crashing through the woods yelling for it to come out. But if we will walk quietly into the woods, sit patiently at the base of a tree, breathe with the earth, and fade into our surroundings, the wild creature we seek might put in an appearance. We may see it only briefly and only out of the corner of an eye—but the sight is a gift we will always treasure as an end in itself.[24]

The soul is a *wild animal.* Something about Palmer's metaphor simultaneously attracts and scares the hell out of me. For so many years I have tried to trap and kill my wild animal because it frightened me—it's uncontrollable. I don't know where it will lead. Is this wild animal the dark side, the shadow side that Jung talks about and Billy helped show me?

The dying have taught me the importance of finding and connecting with my own soul while I am still living. But that's easier said than done.

SOUL SEARCHING

Some of our wisest spiritual guides have pointed out that many spiritual goals cannot be achieved by direct pursuit. For example, in the Christian classic *The Celebration of Discipline,* Richard Foster writes, "Humility, as we all know, is one of those virtues that is never gained by seeking it. The more we pursue it the more distant it becomes."[25] Foster contends that humility comes as a byproduct of serving others.

Similarly, if we want to connect with our soul, we can't, as Palmer says, "go crashing through the woods yelling for it to come out." Noise and commotion seem to chase our souls away, making them harder to find.

Finding and befriending our souls is not easy work. It takes time and effort. Palmer suggests we must "sit patiently at the base of a tree, breathe with the earth." Sitting patiently speaks to me about the need to quiet myself and simply listen.

Meditating, getting quiet, and sitting are time-honored spiritual practices from a variety of faith traditions. I've tried each of these forms, but I've learned that what works best for me is what I call *sensory sitting.* In sensory sitting, I try to engage all my senses. So early in the morning, I grab a cup of coffee, light some incense, sit in a comfortable chair overlooking Pompadour Butte, and watch the sunrise. I often put on some music I like—perhaps Gregorian chants or, better yet, a soundtrack of howling wind. (With the sound of the wind, I imagine I'm Elijah, who was hiding in a cave when God called out to him—see 1 Kings 19:1–18.)

In this practice, I engage each of my senses: the coffee for taste, the incense for smell, the music for hearing, the view for sight, and the comfortable chair for touch. Often I start my time by reading some devotional material to "warm up" my soul, like stretching out before a time of exercise. Then I just sit and wait. I try not to think about *anything in particular,* but I also try *not to think* about anything in particular.

Now, truth be told, some mornings I fall asleep in my comfortable chair. On those mornings I figure I just need more sleep. But, honestly, on most days I look forward to this time. It's not drudgery. I know this is no ascetic practice, but my goal is long-term consistency in getting in touch with my soul and with my God.

I share my own practice with you not so much because I believe you should copy it, but to encourage you to be creative in finding a method of connecting with your soul that works for you.

Thomas Moore has observed that "the soul appears most easily in those places where we feel most inferior."[26] I find this to be true for me. But more importantly, as I sit in my emotional nakedness and honestly reflect on my own wounded soul, it is there that the awful grace of God frequently comes and provides the life-giving, healing balm of acceptance I thirst for. There I find the acceptance I always longed for from my father (who just couldn't express it in the way I wanted). I am covered with the love of God and feel safe and warm in the midst of my flawed silliness. My mornings of sitting alone patiently help ground me for the day (and, I hope, I will be less likely to piss people off). I experience the miracle of being reconciled not only to my own hidden soul but to a loving God.

As I shared earlier, I believe our life experiences can cause us to grow estranged from God, from others, and from ourselves. And I have learned that the remedy to this broken condition is not a linear process. It's not *step one,* get connected to God; *step two,* accept yourself; *step three,* now you can truly love others. My own spiritual journey toward wisdom and compassion has taught me that the road to reconciliation takes a circuitous route. We humans are very complex; trying to unravel the threads of connection to God, self, and others is impossible. We're a tangle. Better stated, we're like a beautifully crafted Persian rug. If we try to pull the threads apart, we'll ruin the beauty of the carpet.

Spiritual growth is often two steps forward, one step back. Truly, as I get more connected to God, I am more able to accept myself and love others. But it is also true that the experience of loving others will feed my love for God and myself. The love of God, self, and others are not stages we progress through, but rather streams along the way that flow into one another.

THE ARTIST

The first time I visited with Juanita, I was with my friend Marianne, who is a social worker. Sometimes these joint visits work out really well for us on the hospice team and for the patient. This was one of those occasions.

When a person signs up for hospice service, the first week can be quite daunting. Federal regulations allow only a short window in which the members of the hospice team are to make contact with the new patient. So it is not unusual for a new hospice patient to receive initial calls from a nurse, a social worker, a chaplain, a home health aide, and a volunteer coordinator within the first few days. Now, imagine you have just been given a terminal diagnosis and are still trying to get your head around the shock to your emotional system when all these calls start coming in. It can be pretty hard to deal with.

So joint visits from members of the hospice team can help alleviate this overwhelming situation. In addition to helping conserve the energy of the patient as he or she works to be hospitable, joint visits can free us on the team to see and learn things we might miss by ourselves.

For example, as Marianne was asking Juanita about her life history and familial relationships—the same questions I often ask in an effort to get to know a patient—I was free to just listen. As I looked around her small mobile home, I noticed it was sparely furnished. Much of what she owned was stacked in boxes in the living room. But then I noticed a framed cartoon-like picture on her living room wall. It was a rather odd image of a large cat with claws extended and a mouth twisted into a snarl that was rushing toward what appeared to be an inflatable cat sitting on a pillow. The inflatable cat was covered in Band-Aids, as if it had been attacked before.

I asked Juanita about the picture and she told us she had painted it. "It's how I feel about talking to plastic people," she explained. "It's not one of my best."

For the next hour, Marianne and I sat mesmerized as this frail woman shaking from the effects of end-stage Parkinson's showed us photos of hundreds of paintings she'd done. All deeply emotional. All slightly odd. All captivating.

These paintings were a window into Juanita's soul. Despite the ridicule of a condescending art teacher and years of marriage to an abusive alcoholic husband, Juanita's soul survived. It had been oppressed, suppressed, and repressed, but it was alive and well. It found a way to communicate itself through her art and we—Marianne and I—were the richer for it.

The Invitation to Now

■

Those who are unhappy have no need for anything in this world but people capable of giving them their attention. The capacity to give one's attention to a sufferer is a very rare and difficult thing; it is almost a miracle; it is a miracle.

—Simone Weil, *Waiting for God*

When I first laid eyes on Ollie, four aides were escorting him to a recliner in the lounge area of the memory-care center. He was very tall, the picture of strong Scandinavian bloodlines, and had enormous calloused hands—trophies of a hard-working life. Taking baby steps on legs that didn't work very well any longer required the assistance of four aides.

I generally am not comfortable in memory-care units because they remind me of images of a turn-of-the-century sanitarium. You've seen those old black-and-white movies of people with disheveled hair running around screaming, or curled up laughing hysterically by themselves, or giving speeches to invisible masses—pretty creepy stuff. Memory-care units tend to be all too much like that, only in living color, not black and white.

Ollie was safely ensconced in a recliner by the time I got to him and tried to introduce myself. He scowled at me, having no idea who I was or what I wanted. Since I have a very low tolerance for rejection, I was about to push off to my next appointment when I recalled what Ollie's wife, Verda, had told me when I'd spoken with her earlier that morning. I remembered her imploring tone as she told me about Ollie's Lutheran faith from former years. I'd heard the hope in her voice that maybe I could make a connection to the man she'd loved for more than fifty years who now resided somewhere in this memoryless body.

So I did what I usually do when I feel uncomfortable: I sat there with my mouth shut. I decided I could at least pray for this dear man who was suffering from the dreaded disease of dementia. At first, I tried to pray silently with my eyes closed. But after a few seconds, the noise of the unit and my fear of being attacked by an out-of-control crazy person caused me to open my eyes again, for safety's sake.

On the other side of the room, an aide was using a curling iron to beautify the hair of an elderly woman in a wheelchair holding a toy baby doll. A little brown-and-black dog was running around, harmlessly inspecting everything. There was also a little woman in a sweat suit curled up on a sofa trying to get comfortable and take a nap.

I started praying again (this time with my eyes open) and began to look at Ollie, the subject of my prayers. I sought to look at him mindfully, to really see him—who he is now, this tall gentle giant sitting in a recliner in front of me in this particular time and place. I became fascinated with him. Ollie was wearing a checked green polo shirt and was using those enormous hands to pick the lint out of the breast pocket. He had the whole pocket turned inside out and kept picking and picking at the lint. Little bits of torn tissue paper were all over his lap, yet he kept picking.

As I watched his methodical work, I decided to try entering his world and told him he was doing a great job. Ollie looked up and smiled at me. Amazingly, Ollie's smile helped me to relax and at the same time felt like an invitation to play along. I became Ollie's cheerleader, and he started laughing.

During the next few moments, I felt a deep connection with this demented elderly man in the green polo shirt who was obsessively picking lint out of his breast pocket. I started to imagine what storyline Ollie was telling himself about what he was doing. Why was getting the lint out so important? That's when I remembered that I hadn't slept much the previous night because I kept replaying in my mind, over and over again, a conversation I'd had the day before with another patient. During that meeting, I'd made a hurtful comment, and I'd perseverated about that stupid comment all night long—planning what I could say to apologize, making excuses for my inconsiderate behavior, and imagining what she might say and how I might respond. It was mental nit-picking, just like Ollie's digging for lint in his breast pocket. Ollie and I had more in common than I thought.

That afternoon, Ollie taught me several important life lessons. First, if you want to connect with someone new, try entering into his world before asking him to help you complete your agenda. Second, while a person might look like a total alien, if you stop and really are present with that person, you may discover you have more in common than you ever imagined. The third lesson I learned from Ollie is perhaps the most important, and it's one my patients continue to teach me. It's about the importance of living in the present moment—what the Zen folks call *mindfulness*.

MISSING THE CUES

Sometimes the lessons I learn from my patients can be quite unpleasant. When I first met Charlene, she was in an assisted-living facility and had been lying on her bed in pain for more than an hour when I arrived. She'd been experiencing bowel problems, and her bathroom had feces all over the floor. After forty-five minutes and two calls to the front desk, her aide arrived with some medication to alleviate Charlene's suffering and clean the mess in the bathroom. On that first visit I simply sat holding Charlene's hand, telling stories and trying to distract us both from her pain and the smell until help could arrive.

Several weeks later I wanted to follow up to see how she was doing, so I stopped by her apartment, without phoning first to ask if I could visit. When I knocked on her door and announced who I was, I heard her clearly say, "Today is not a good day. Come back another time." But I was having trouble scheduling my visits that week, and I was already in the building to see another patient. So I opened her door to just peek in, if only so I could claim the stop as a visit that would count toward my weekly quota. Charlene barked at me, "I said this wasn't a good day, and I don't want to see you today!"

I quickly closed the door and left—but the feeling of shame didn't. I had violated Charlene's autonomy so that I could attend to my own compulsiveness in performing well and completing my assigned duties for the week. Worse, I was treating this woman like a chore. As I sat in my car to drive away, the uneasiness in my gut told me that I'd overstepped a real boundary with Charlene.

Reflecting further on this incident, I realized I never would have intruded on Charlene if I had been more mindful, if I'd paid attention in the moment to what was really being said and what was going on. I had allowed my fears about my scheduling difficulties for the week and the possibility of having a poor performance review to harm the possibility of Charlene and I having a respectful continued relationship. The embarrassment I felt in the car driving away was a painful reminder to pay attention to the people I am with in the moment—to really see them, really hear them, really respect them.

THE FREEDOM NOW OFFERS

Fortunately, my mindfulness lessons aren't always so painful.

Phil was a pleasant reminder of the importance of living mindfully. On the day I first met him, Phil was lying in his recliner, surrounded by his wife, daughter, and grandson. Phil had been some kind of engineer in his working days, but he was a philosopher at heart. For example, Phil told me he thought God didn't put us here on earth so God could make us happy but put us here to make ourselves happy.

During my initial interview with Phil, he told me he loved to sit in his recliner and look at the beauty of nature out his window. He described with poetic insight the trees and hummingbirds and change of light as the sun set. While all that was nice, Phil really caught me when he said, "You know, after I got my diagnosis, I was really grateful. Now I can enjoy every moment without worrying about tomorrow."

Phil's words reminded me of a famous Zen *koan*.

One day an old man was walking through the hills looking for blueberries when a hungry mountain lion caught his scent. On hearing the lion, the old man took off running. As he ran, he ran out of room. In no time flat he found himself at the edge of a massive cliff. Looking over the cliff, he saw a drop of about a hundred feet with all kinds of jagged rocks at the bottom. With the mountain lion closing in fast, the old man spied a tree vine, grabbed it, and swung out over the edge of the cliff. He ended up hanging about ten feet down from the cliff's edge.

So there he was hanging on for dear life. When he looked up, he saw the mountain lion baring its teeth and licking its lips waiting for a warm meal. When he looked down, he saw the jagged rocks. Then, out of the corner of his eye, the old man noticed a strawberry bush growing right out of the face of the cliff with the biggest reddest strawberry he'd ever seen. Clinging to the vine with one hand, he reached out with the other hand to grab the strawberry. He ate it and said, "Yum, that's the best strawberry I ever ate."

That's it. That's the *koan*.

As it was explained to me, the brilliance of the old man in the story is that he didn't allow the fears of his past (the mountain lion) or the fears of his future (the rocks below) to rob him from the here-and-now opportunity to enjoy the best strawberry he'd ever eaten. That's mindfulness.

Mindfulness liberates us from past and future fears. And that affords us the opportunity to live in the present with courageous compassion.

THE EYES HAVE IT

Harriett was another patient who offered me a big red strawberry. She was just a little bag of bones lying on a bed in the back room of an adult foster home. Her caregivers had told me Harriett had been a Baptist, but the folks from her church had stopped visiting long ago. Harriett could no longer talk, and the disease process had atrophied her legs so they were folded up like a pretzel—but her big brown eyes were always open and seemed to dance.

Harriett's nurse told me that Harriett liked it when people sang to her. Now, that's way out of my comfort zone. I sing in the key of K9—I howl like a dog. I couldn't find a tune with a road map. But discarding all my feelings of self-consciousness, I sang to Harriett. I tried to think of good Baptist songs and came up with "Jesus Loves Me This I Know." Singing that song made me feel like a little kid again. Who cares if I can't sing? I'm going to anyway! And Harriett's eyes just danced.

My last visit with Harriett was very different. Her eyes were no longer dancing; they looked vacant. I must have sat there for at least twenty minutes just looking into her eyes—I mean really staring. I wanted to really see her, who she was. I prayed for her and reassured her that she was in a safe place, but mostly I just looked into those eyes. It was an intensely intimate visit, and it opened up wells of emotion deep inside me. I realized my own humanity on a new level. Yes, there are now seven billion of us on this rock, individuals all, but Harriett taught me that in some unseen way we're all connected—all part of one another.

Twelve hours later Harriett died.

In his book *Soul Prints,* Marc Gafni tells a story about going to see a mystical rabbi in Jerusalem. Gafni explains that it was difficult to get an appointment with this particular rabbi because he would meet with folks only for a few hours each day, and those meetings were generally in the middle of the night. So at 3 or 4 in the morning, Gafni met this little Russian man. Here's how he relates the encounter.

> During the entire time in which you are in his presence, he is fully focused on your face. For the forty-five minutes I sat with him, he was absolutely intent upon me. His eyes did not waver. Not only did he refrain from looking at his watch, but it was clearly apparent that the only thing he was thinking about were the words I was saying. For him in that moment, my utterances were the most important thing in the entire world. When I left, I didn't take with me any great advice or a solution to the particular problem that I had brought to him. However, I did leave feeling fully received, and somehow that itself was the answer.[27]

Maya Angelou said, "I've learned that people will forget what you said, people will forget what you did, but people will never forget how you made them feel."

In my own self-scripting memory of being with Harriett, I imagine I was the little Russian rabbi for Harriett, or an embodiment of Maya Angelou's insight. But the truth is, sitting with Harriett taught me how wonderful it can be to forget about my own neurotic self for a little while and simply get absorbed in being with someone else. Listening to another. Seeing another. Not being the center of the universe for a few short moments can be so freeing—so relaxing.

Finally, there is a very practical benefit from practicing mindfulness in this way with patients: it forestalls getting burned out. Mother Teresa used to remind her co-workers in Calcutta that they could not fix the problems of the people they served. We can't cure the cancer; we can't make an old body young; we can't breathe new life into damaged lungs. But we can bear witness to the suffering. We can really see the living person, the human being. We can acknowledge their struggle. We can hold their hand, cry with them, pray for them, encourage them, assure them they are in a safe place—and in so doing we help sanctify the experience for them and ourselves. And this is enough.

The Meaning of Life

■

Humans are creators of meaning, and finding deep meaning in our experiences is not just another name for spirituality but it is also the very shape of human happiness.

—Richard Rohr, *Falling Upward*

This nursing home, like most nursing homes, smelled of old people and stale urine. Over the years I've learned to carry a small cylindrical inhaler of lavender scent to ward off the repugnant aromas. After a couple of refreshing whiffs, I found Mary's room.

Mary was lying on her bed, flat on her back, asleep. On the other side of the sheer curtain that divided the room in half was a family in the process of admitting a new patient.

At the foot of the new patient's bed, I could see the TV was turned on to one of those shopping channels, or maybe it was one of those demonic infomercials. On the screen, a cherubic woman with curly red hair was hawking the new and improved Express ReadySetGo cooking pan. I watched as she placed little Vienna sausages in the compartments while some old white guy next to her on the set looked on in utter amazement, as if she were spinning lead into gold. With the sound muted, you could see just how stupid the whole product was—an item to be sold for fifty cents at some future garage sale.

Among the family members gathered with the new patient was an older man who was complaining about how far away they'd had to park. He said his feet were hurting from the walk. The patient's granddaughter was on her cell phone, calling the doctor's office and demanding the names of the medications her grandmother was taking so they could inform the nursing home staff. A middle-aged man was talking to the new patient, who was thrashing around on the bed. "Now don't try 'n get up, Ma," he cooed in a sickeningly patronizing manner. "You'll only hurt yourself."

I finally tore myself away from the drama playing out behind the curtain and focused again on Mary. The first thing I noticed was her incredibly large triangular nose. It looked almost like one of those fake noses that came attached to thick black plastic glasses and furry eyebrows, and although it was perfectly triangular, one nostril was bigger than the other.

I began to wonder what Mary was like as a young woman. Whom had she loved? What had she hoped for? What were the things that made her heart flutter and her face flush?

After Mary woke up and I tried to introduce myself, she dove into a long monologue about how she had to get some rest before a long afternoon of cooking a big Christmas dinner with all of the fixings for her family. Mary's body had been bed-bound in the nursing home for many months, but her mind was somewhere else. As I listened to Mary describing her plans for the day, I began to wonder if her Christmas dinner delusion was a defense mechanism to protect her from the pain of being a bed-ridden prisoner in a smelly nursing home, an escape to a time when life was filled with meaning.

Do I do the same thing? Do I create elaborate scenarios in my mind to make sense of the pain in my own reality? Do I seek comfort in a soothing sense of meaning?

LOOKING FOR A PLACE TO FIT

As I've been working on this book and teaching the material in several different venues, one theme that has emerged surrounds the self-scripting we all do. Thich Nhat Hahn calls these scripts "mental formations."

It works like this. I walk into the coffee room at the office where everyone has been laughing and yucking it up. Upon my arrival, the laughing stops and folks go back to work. My internal scriptwriter begins immediately. *They were laughing at you. Your clothes look funny today. You've put on weight.* Or any one of a million other me-centered explanations for what just took place. In reality, the cessation of laughter might have had nothing to do with me at all. But my self-scripting mental formations don't care—they keep right on creating explanations for what just took place, usually with me in a negative light.

Another major project for this internal scribe involves our deep-seated desire to find meaning for our existence. Our egos work overtime to find a meta-narrative we can plug into to help make sense of our personal life story. Once it's found, we begin to write a script that makes sense of the world and our unique place in it. Simply put, each of us is looking for a place to fit.

For some, this meta-narrative might be the Christian story and living a life to help advance the kingdom of God. For others, including those following the Buddhist tradition, it might involve playing an active role in alleviating the suffering of other sentient beings. For many others, it means working in pursuit of the American Dream and providing a safe, nurturing place for one's family to get ahead.

Philosophers have observed that this obsessive existential search for meaning so common in our culture today has been more acute during the past several hundred years. Prior to that, not so much. Our ancestors don't seem to have been as concerned about the meaning of life. Maybe the primal fight simply to stay alive—fighting off enemies, plagues, starvation, and the elements—required so much effort that there was little time left over for intense introspection on questions such as "Why am I here?"

Be that as it may, in my practice as a hospice chaplain, there is no more pressing work than helping patients reframe their sense of meaning at the end of their lives. The reason is simple: the most frequent spiritual pain I encounter is loss of meaning. So many people I meet are more afraid of losing their meaning than they are of dying.

The existential pain inflicted by the loss of meaning is often exacerbated by the degree to which the dying must confront our cultural idol of independence. The last thing anyone in North America wants is to be dependent on another. So for the dying person, who often can find no reason to continue living, the thought of being a burden to their loved ones and requiring care that uses the family's resources of time and money is unbearably painful. This is suffering that pharmaceuticals can't touch. This is soul suffering.

As a chaplain, I seek to help alleviate this soul suffering in several ways. First, by bearing witness to it. Suffering often isolates the sufferer, which only intensifies the pain. As I have sat patiently with the persons who are dying, honestly talking in nonjudgmental ways about their loss of meaning and fear of being a burden to others, I have witnessed a lessoning of this excruciating existential pain. Simply naming it, looking at it square in the eye, and not running from it have incredible therapeutic value.

THE GAMBLER

Irene called one afternoon and asked if I could come visit Walter right away, because he wanted "to give his life to the Lord." Now in the evangelical world, this is code language for getting "saved." I was glad to oblige.

Walter had just been discharged from the hospital into hospice care and was now living at home. He had lost more that forty pounds during the previous month due to esophageal cancer and the chemotherapy used to treat it. The radiation had burned his esophagus so thoroughly he lost the ability to eat. His wife, Irene, who loved both Walter and the Lord, wanted to make sure the two of them met.

I remember the first words out of Walter's mouth were, "If I could put a bullet in my head right now, I'd end it all—but I love her too much to do it." "Her" was Irene.

Walter and Irene had been together for seventeen years, a second marriage for both. He told me his first marriage had lasted forty-plus years, "but it was just companionship. What I have with Irene is deep love." Walter tearfully shared that his only reason for wanting to stay alive was because he knew that, without his benefits, Irene (who was legally blind) would lose their home.

He survived for three more months on this deep love.

Walter did pray to become a Christian during my first visit with him. After that, he cried all the time. Despite having such difficulty in swallowing, amazing grace entered his soul. Over the course of our visits, Walter told me he'd struggled with a gambling problem for many years, running up huge debts. At one point Irene said she'd leave him if he didn't quit gambling. He quit. Deep love is powerful stuff.

For her part, Irene was incredible. She cared for this man 24/7 by herself. As he continued to decline, she helped him keep his skin clean to avoid its breaking down and causing wounds. Because of her blindness, she had to put her nose to his butt to make sure he was properly cleaned. Deep love.

Walter struggled with being bedridden, unable to taste food (and later, unable to eat at all), having lost all meaning for his living save the benefits he provided for Irene. But he told me just talking about it out loud helped ease the pain. "It's funny," he shared, "talking doesn't change it one bit, but when you come I do feel better." I've learned that bearing witness to suffering breaks its isolation.

About a month before Walter died, Irene consented to let a friend drive him to a casino about a hundred miles away. One last fling. Walter went. Of course he lost some money, but he had a great time.

He told me near the end that he had no regrets about his life. He felt so fortunate to have found Irene, and they'd been able to enjoy the years they had with each other. Walter had gambled on deep love—and won.

PILGRIM'S PROGRESS

Another way I seek to help soothe the soul suffering of those in hospice care is to explore possibilities of reframing meaning for the end of life. Okay, you can't pay the bills anymore, or feed the grandchildren, but how can you still be a dad? A grandmother? How can you still contribute to the emotional welfare of your loved ones? We'll explore some of these possibilities more in a little while, but for now, it is enough just to acknowledge the importance of the questions.

Before we can begin to answer these questions, we must remember that our understanding of our life's meaning is inextricably intertwined with the story we've created to make sense of our existence. Our stories tell us where we fit in this world. *Remember:* We are formed by the stories we tell ourselves; if we want to change our behavior, we have to change the story. To reframe the meaning of our lives requires rewriting the old story or creating a new one. And that story usually revolves around two central poles: our relationships and our roles.

Sitting next to Jake's bed as he lay dying, watching his fitful sleep, I noticed the framed sign on the wall near his bed in the adult foster home. It read: "When I was a kid, I prayed every night for a bicycle, but then I found out this isn't the way God works. So then I stole one and asked Him for forgiveness."

A hard life of drugs, alcohol, and rock-n-roll had taken its toll on Jake's forty-something-year-old body. Contrary to the conventional wisdom, living fast and dying young doesn't always leave a good-looking corpse. Nearly all of Jake's teeth had rotted out, save the bicuspid on his upper right side. His abdomen was greatly distended (bloated) from terminal liver disease. And Jake was painfully afraid of death.

Jake had some sort of a Baptist background, and had loved to play the drums. Years before, as a result of his addictions, Jake had deserted his wife and daughter. When I first met him, he told me that all he wanted was to see them again, to be given a last chance to "make things right." Mercifully, his ex-wife and daughter did come to see him, bringing along a newborn grandson whom Jake had never seen. It was a beautiful reunion with a lot of love and grace. Before they left, Jake's family made a collage of family pictures and mounted it on the wall next to the framed sign. Jake was so proud of his family. He would lie for hours on his side, simply looking at the collage and delighting in the pictures of his grandson.

But now, weeks later, he was dying, and I was sitting there praying for him. Several times he woke up in pain. His caregiver, Joe, and I repositioned him to ease his way. I moistened his lips and mouth with one of those pink sponge swabs soaked in water.

Looking at the pictures of his daughter and grandson, I thought of how much Jake had missed out on as he wandered the world looking for his place to fit. What if everything his thirsty soul had longed for was right there at home the whole time?

Earlier that morning, I'd read some lines from Antony the Great, the first of the desert fathers. "What must one do in order to please God? Pay attention to what I tell you. Whoever you may be, always have God before your eyes. Whatever you do, do according to the testimony of the Holy Scriptures. Wherever you live, do not easily leave it. Keep these three precepts, and you will be saved."[28]

We're all looking for a place to fit. We're all looking for a metanarrative, a grand story that helps explain our lives, makes sense of our existence, and provides a source of meaning to our days. Often, we don't need to travel to discover that story. I think that's why St. Antony tells us that, if we find that place, we should not easily leave it.

I was still lost in these thoughts when Joe the caregiver's two young daughters arrived home from school and went running down the hallway outside of Jake's door fighting about something. I said a short benediction for Jake and bade him Godspeed.

As I pulled out of the driveway, I noticed in the rearview mirror two young Mormon missionaries cresting the hill behind me. Their starched white shirts and black ties were a sharp contrast to the gray overcast November sky behind them. *Two more pilgrims searching for a place to fit,* I thought. Aren't we all?

Healing in Hospice

■

There will, I hope, still be opportunities to go on trips, play with the kids, do the dishes, pay the bills, listen to music, help with the homework, attend a couple of football games, go to movies, do a little bit of writing, share happy moments with my wife and family, renew friendships with some people and reach closure with others, search for spiritual meaning in and acceptance of the life I have lived, and search for healing even in the absence of cure.

—Dr. Paul Cazier ("Stealing the Reaper's Grim: The Challenge of Dying Well," voicing his hope as he was dying from a cancerous brain tumor)

My first experience in observing the intense pain caused by a loss of meaning occurred long before my career as a chaplain began. It came from watching my mother die.

I was just in my early twenties and my mom was only forty-four. She had battled cancer for seven years. It started in her breast, and then went to the ovaries, then, finally and painfully, into her bones. Double mastectomy, chemo, radiation, the indignity of all her beautiful black hair falling out, her caring face mooning up from the medications—none of it worked. For the last year of her life, she basically lay in constant pain on the couch in our family room and had to let my three sisters, my father, and I take care of her.

Her greatest pain, however, was not being able "to be our mom" anymore. She often told me she hated having everyone wait on her. She felt like such a burden to us. Throughout our lives, she had cared for and nurtured us. Now she could only lie on that damn couch.

I remember one evening during her last year when she and I were home alone. I was lying on the floor in the family room watching TV, and she asked me, "Do you want some ice cream?" Half jokingly, I said, "Yeah, right."

A short while later she labored to get up off of the sofa, grabbed her crutches, and started up the seven stairs from the family room to the rest of the house. I thought she was just going to the bathroom. She returned a few minutes later, gingerly balancing a bowl of ice cream in her right hand as she cautiously made her way back down the stairs. I felt so ashamed, yet she looked so happy. She told me that, for just a few moments, she felt like a mom again.

While a very difficult life experience, those were some of the richest moments in my life. I had just graduated from college and moved home to help care for her. Those last several months of tending to my mother were an opportunity for me to give back to this beautiful woman who had given me and our family so much of herself. Serving her pulled a kindness and sensitivity out of me that I didn't even know was there. I was a better human being as a result of those months attending to my dying mother.

Ironically, letting us serve her as she was dying was the final gift our mother gave us. Her care filled *our* lives with deep meaning.

Now I'm not suggesting it was easy, or that it made us happy, but it did make our living very rich. Not infrequently I share this insight with those I serve who also suffer from a loss of meaning as they lay dying. I suggest that even confined to the hospital bed, unable to care for themselves in any way, the dying patient can still teach the rest of the family how meaningful life can be as we serve others.

Nearly forty years later, the impact of those months has never left me. The experience of serving my dying mother was a major consideration in my life choice to become a hospice chaplain.

HEALING VERSUS CURE

As we work on this task to create meaning and discover "who we really are," we need the skill of *reflection*. The word "reflection" has two primary meanings in English—to see ourselves as in a mirror, and also to look inward in a contemplative way.[29]

In my own search for meaning, I've found the two to be intimately connected. Philosophers (particularly the existentialist ones like Heidegger and Sartre) believe it's impossible to know ourselves apart from being in relationship. The existentialists teach it is by getting feedback from others about who we are (mirror reflection) that we can then truly look inward to contemplate our being (contemplative reflection). "By linking ourselves (who can't be very objective) with others (who can be more so), we gain access to ourselves."[30] Therefore, the only way I can truly come to know myself and create any sense of meaning is by being in relationship with others.

I think this in large part why I'm so driven to find a group to fit in with—a group that shares my worldview and experiences. This thirst for identifying with a group manifests every weekend during football season here in Oregon, as in Ducks versus Beavers. Or Packers versus Bears. It goes on further into Democrats versus Republicans. Protestants versus Catholics. MSNBC versus Fox.

The reality is this—what you and I are really looking to discover is *ourselves*. We align with a group that reflects back to us the "we" that we want to be.

Therefore, in this work of meaning-making, the importance of our roles and relationships cannot be overstated. John Pilch, in his insightful work, *Healing in the New Testament,* does a masterful job of differentiating cure from healing.[31] Cure is a medical term that speaks of eliminating a spot from an X-ray, or cutting out diseased tissue, or using pharmaceuticals to destroy unwanted bacteria. Healing, on the other hand, requires a much broader understanding. Healing may involve cure, but it also includes restoring the sick person to his or her familial relationships and roles in the broader community when needed.

In the Palestine of the first century, sick people were often quarantined to limit the spread of dreaded diseases like leprosy. Diseased folks were often segregated, forced to live at the margins of the community, and required to yell "unclean" if others approached to keep healthy people at a safe distance. Folks with certain diseases weren't permitted to live in their own homes, engage in commerce with local merchants, or go to work. These conditions increased the isolation and suffering of the afflicted persons.

This is the reason, Pilch points out, Jesus frequently told people he healed to "go show yourself to the priest." Showing oneself to the priest was the gateway back into the life of the community. Once you were no longer deemed unclean (that is, a threat to the welfare of the larger community), you could move back into your home to resume your role as mother or father relationally, and you could go back to work to resume your role in helping the entire community survive. This is the biblical meaning of healing.

Thus one can be healed without obtaining a cure. Pilch adds a further insight: "Healing is also effective when the individual experience of illness has been made meaningful, personal suffering shared, and the individual leaves the marginal situation of sickness and is reincorporated—in health or even death—back into the social body."[32]

I like to say that our cure rate in hospice work runs at about zero percent, but we're pretty good at healing. How is this accomplished?

UPON FURTHER REFLECTION

In my work to help dying persons recover a sense of meaning at the end of their lives, I rely on several approaches to help patients reframe meaning given their current terminal circumstances. First, I try to reflect back to them the beauty I see in them. In understanding my own role as an agent of religion I want to offer them what God has always offered to me—loving acceptance. My hope is that with a real sense of being accepted the dying person will be encouraged to continue the sometimes scary task of inner reflection.

Next I share with them what they've taught me. Now, this must be something very particular and real—not just something that sounds pretty or kind or spiritual. This is no time for Blowing Smoke. Dying patients have a keen smell for B.S. Again, I want to reflect back to the person a positive image of not just who he or she was, but who that person is now, to aid in the important work of self-contemplation.

Nurse Pam could hardly contain her laughter as she told me our new patient Amos wanted to see me. Amos didn't fit the usual profile of a hospice patient wanting spiritual support.

My first visit lasted an hour and a half and felt like a test. Amos dropped more F-bombs and smoked more cigarettes than I could count. I learned he'd spent a lot of years in prison, had knifed several folks, was an enforcer for mobsters, and liked to read detective stories. When he saw he couldn't scare me off, he eased up.

Over the next several weeks he told wild stories from his life and introduced me to colorful aphorisms like, "Don't let your alligator mouth overload your hummingbird ass."

I introduced him to Jack Reacher.

He told me about how hard it was growing up. How his father used to beat him, then when he was ten, his dad just up and left. On his twenty-first birthday, Amos got drunk, found his dad, and beat the shit out of him. "Greatest day of my life," he said.

But underneath all the F-bombs, cigarette smoke, and stories of prison life, Amos had a softer side. He told me how he had met Rena (his now deceased wife) and how his love for her changed him. "Until I met her, I never did anything that wasn't selfish. . . . But she taught me how to love. She taught me how to think of others. She taught me how to be kind."

His disease process worsened, and, as Amos couldn't walk anymore or do anything but read his crime novels, his frustration grew more intense. One day as we were talking, Amos was again bitching about his life, his crummy apartment, and the fact that he was dying and I just interrupted him. I don't know why but I just began to tell him what he had taught me over the weeks. I told him how moved I was by his love for Rena and how it gave me hope that it's never too late to change your life. As I went on he looked like a little kid in rapt attention. Better, he looked like a flower whose petals were opening up in time-lapse photography. I was simply reflecting back parts of him that he had trouble seeing anymore. It eased his pain, for a while.

Amos became a good friend and a great teacher. Amos taught me the power of positive reflection.

MAY YOU FIND SOME COMFORT HERE

Other techniques I've learned to help alleviate existential end-of-life pain include suggesting that patients teach their loved ones how to die. This is particularly appropriate for dying parents and grandparents. They've already given much of their lives to teaching their progeny how to live; now they can teach them how to die. This approach reinforces the dying person's role in the family structure, and it also provides a wonderful gift, because so many folks in our culture are terrified of death. Teaching others to die without fear, without regret, is an incredible gift. Henri Nouwen wrote,

> If I die with much anger and bitterness, I will leave my family and friends behind in confusion, guilt, shame, or weakness. When I felt my death approaching, I suddenly realized how much I could influence the hearts of those whom I would leave behind. If I could truly say that I was grateful for what I had lived, eager to forgive and be forgiven, full of hope that those who loved me would continue their lives in joy and peace, and confident that Jesus who calls me would guide all who somehow belonged to my life—if I could do that—I would, in the hour of my death, reveal more true spiritual freedom than I had been able to reveal all the years of my life. I realized on a very deep level that dying is the most important act of living. It involves a choice to bind others with guilt or set them free with gratitude.[33]

I find Nouwen's insight incredibly inspirational. How beautifully rich it can be to teach those you love how to die. In a world that offers so much impersonal social media, plastic gizmos, and answers for everything, sharing the vulnerable uncertainties of the dying process is such an intimate invitation to love. It can also be a powerful source of meaning to help dying persons endure the numerous indignities involved with residing in a body that is simply giving out.

Another approach to reframing meaning as one approaches death is to consider how the dying person might *bless* his or her loved ones. In *The Gift of the Blessing,* Gary Smalley and John Trent draw on biblical material to identify five basic elements in an effective blessing: meaningful touch, spoken words, expressing high value, picturing a special future, and offering an active commitment to see that future becomes reality.[34] Helping dying patients consider how they might want to bless their loved ones in casual or more ritualized ways provides a rich vein of possibilities laden with meaning. Simply noticing and celebrating the special lives of those who surround them is a simple and beautiful gift that dying persons can offer to those whom they love.

Finally, with some of my patients, I emphasize the gift of receiving care from others. As I shared in the story about my mother's dying, by letting me help care for her, my mother allowed me to discover gifts within me I didn't know I had—gifts like kindness and tenderness. Some people find it incredibly difficult to receive, but doing so can afford those who love you an opportunity to express their love in creative and tangible ways—ways that may change the giver forever.

But helping to provide a measure of healing for hospice patients doesn't always require direct interventions like those I've just shared. Sometimes all that is required is simply to show up.

A VACATION FROM DYING

Some folks I visit just want a vacation from the dying process. Such was the case with two sisters I fell in love with, Elaine and Gigi—"the girls." Elaine, the patient, had some form of cancer. She and her sister both smoked like fiends, and both were suffering from mild dementia. Between the two of them you couldn't put together one good working memory.

My weekly visits with the sisters always took place out on the back deck of their mobile home, where the girls smoked. Gigi always put her name on her pack of cigarettes, even though they both smoked the same brand and stole each other's cigarettes constantly.

Elaine had always been the one to balance the checkbooks for both, but as her condition worsened, she couldn't keep up. This created its own stress.

I always made sure they were my last visit of the day, because after the visit my clothes reeked of stale cigarettes. But I loved going there. Elaine had a small white yappy dog named Phoebe who wouldn't leave me alone. So they'd lock the dog up inside the house, we'd sit on the back deck in a cloud of smoke, and we'd just tease, tell stories, and laugh. I can't remember any great insight or specific poignant experience we shared; it was just wonderful being together.

I knew my visits were a break for them. For Elaine, it was a break from thinking about the progress of the cancer growing in her body, lamenting her diminishing capacities, and worrying about who would take care of Gigi and Phoebe when she was gone. For Gigi, it was a break from watching her beloved sister shrivel away to death, wrestling with the nagging questions of how she would manage on her own, and worrying about what might happen if she dropped one of the thirty-plus little pills Elaine took daily to control her severe pain and the dog ingested it. My visits were a break from the blaring noise of Judge Joe Brown on television in the background and the long periods of silence when the television was off.

We really didn't talk about anything substantive, yet it was all important. Each visit, we'd tell the same stories, ask the same questions, and laugh again at the silliness of it all. Sometimes not having a good memory can be a blessing.

The girls taught me that you don't have to be wise or insightful to be of help. Sometimes just showing up to provide a few moments of distraction is enough.

WHAT DO I HAVE TO LIVE FOR?

I'd already known Maria for a while when she entered hospice. Her husband of more than sixty years had died on our hospice service the year before. Two years earlier, she and her husband had sold their home and had moved in with her daughter and her family. My first visit with Maria as a hospice patient found her flat on her back in bed. She'd just been diagnosed with stage four cancer and had declined treatment. Maria's refusal to aggressively fight the cancer was particularly hurtful to her daughter, Lily, who took the decision personally. "Does she hate living with us so much that she'd rather die?"

I'll never forget the first words out of Maria's mouth when I entered her room. She looked up at me with huge brown eyes and simply said in her thick Italian accent, "What do I have to live for?" Her words pierced my heart.

As we talked, she spoke about how she'd cared for her husband and their home for the majority of her eighty-plus years. Now, both her husband and her home were gone. The cancer was simply the final blow. She was no longer able to do many of the things she'd enjoyed, such as playing with her great grandchildren. Even though she loved her daughter, the prospects of enduring chemo and radiation to simply sit on her daughter's back porch and smoke cigarettes was more than she could bear.

Maria asked me if it was a sin to decline treatment. "Not in my book," I told her. While that seemed to relieve her, I also encouraged her to tell Lily how much she loved her and explain that her decision to decline aggressive treatments was not based on anything Lily had done. "You don't want to leave your daughter with those nagging questions of 'What did I do wrong?' do you?" Maria agreed.

As I was driving away from their home, Maria's question came back to hit me with penetrating force: "What do I have to live for?" I think every one of us has to face that question for ourselves.

What do I have to live for?

Servant's Entrance

■

Life's most persistent and urgent question is

"What are you doing for others?"

—Martin Luther King Jr.

As I say, loss of meaning is far and away the most frequent spiritual pain I encounter. Patients will often lament, "Why am I still here? Why won't God take me?" The majority of the patients I encounter are more afraid of losing their life's meaning than they are of dying.

Ginny was one of those people. Every time I visited Ginny at her adult foster home, the country music playing in her room was blaring, because of her hearing loss. Ginny told me that she loved her dad but hated her mother. She had worked much of her life in a large upscale department store, and she had resented the snooty wealthy customers she had to serve. "If I'd a hadda gun, I coulda killed 'em, they made me so mad," she told me.

"I'm glad you didn't," I said, "cause I'd hate to have to visit you in prison." Her little eyes squeezed up, her nose crinkled, and she laughed.

Ginny reminded me of my Grandma Stein. Grandma Stein was quite a character. I particularly remember one Christmas nearly thirty years ago when I phoned Grandma Stein and asked what she wanted for her present. Her response really surprised me, "I'm not gonna tell you, because you won't do it."

"Grandma, I'm asking what you want. Tell me."

"I want to go to the wrestling."

Now by "the wrestling," she was referring to the traveling wrestling show that was coming to West Virginia's Wheeling Civic Auditorium. Amused and surprised, I agreed to take her, and even suggested that we go to dinner at Elby's (a Denny's-like restaurant) and make a night of it. She was ecstatic.

A friend got us ringside seats, and it was a hoot. The place was packed with screaming fanatics who had gathered to watch these enormous men fake punch, fake jab, fake scratch, and fake throw themselves all over the ring. At one point, there was a featured match in which an Iranian wrestler was scheduled to battle Sergeant Slaughter (an ex-Marine). Now, this was in 1980, during the Iranian hostage crisis, so the plot of the fight was designed to stir everyone up into patriotic frenzy. To gin up the crowd even more, a Russian wrestler came out in the middle of the bout and illegally teamed up with the Iranian man to beat up Sgt. Slaughter. The place went nuts. Finally, some other good guy wrestlers came out to help Sgt. Slaughter, and they chased the bad guys right out of the arena. Everyone was screaming, including a particularly loud group of teenagers sitting right behind us.

In the middle of all this fake mayhem, Grandma Stein stood up, turned around, and began to cuss out the teenagers, "Shut the hell up!" she yelled, "I'm seventy-six years old, and I don't have to put up with this shit! Now, shut the hell up!" Then she sat back down.

The teenagers sat there in stunned disbelief.

After sitting down, Grandma Stein leaned over to me and whispered, "There's a certain class of people that come to this kind of thing."

That was my Grandma Stein.

Anyway, I don't know if it was her playful feistiness, her offbeat sense of humor, or the cussing—but Ginny reminded me of Grandma Stein.

"All I do is sit in this damn chair and stare out the window. I'm either in the bed or the chair. I'm ninety-six, and this is all I do," Ginny angrily complained. To help alleviate her existential pain, I worked to help Ginny reframe a sense of meaning for this point in her life, confined as she was to her room in an adult foster home. We talked about how caring for her provided the folks employed by the foster home with meaningful work and income, and about how she made them all laugh when they came into her room. I reminded Ginny that she certainly wasn't a snooty customer demanding prompt service like the people she'd worked for years ago at the department store. This image helped Ginny laugh and relax, at least for the moment.

Philosophers say the search for meaning is one of the primary drives of our lives. While they do not all agree on what meaning is, or how to discover it, they agree that the search is universal.

Over the years, I've read quite a bit about what constitutes our sense of meaning. It is strongly impacted by culture, philosophy, and religion. While many people have very strong opinions as to what is the meaning of life, there is no consensus. There are, however, several acknowledged characteristics to living a meaningful life. Each individual discovers life's meaning uniquely; in other words, no one can tell you what it is—it's yours to find. Additionally, life's meaning is dynamic, not static. It changes over the seasons of our lives. What makes life meaningful for someone at age twenty is often not the same when that person reaches age sixty.

Aristotle taught that what everyone wants most is happiness. He contended that happiness is the only thing we humans strive for as an end unto itself. For example, we work to earn money. But we want money to buy things. And we buy things to be happy. We have no other motive for seeking happiness. It and it alone is the goal. But since the days of Aristotle, many philosophers have noted that happiness rarely comes by direct pursuit. More frequently it comes as a result of serving others.

Serving others can be a key element in our quest for lives of meaning. The importance of helping others has only been reinforced by my study of heroic lives like that of the Buddha, Francis, Gandhi, King Jr., Mandela, Mother Teresa, and (most significantly for me) Jesus. The one we call Christ said, "I have not come to be served, but to serve and give my life away for those who are held hostage." (Matthew 10:28 MSG)

Serving others—that is, taking action on behalf of another person's interests rather than our own—is a sure sign of an authentic spiritual practice. Why? Because we're all interconnected. Trusted voices like Merton, Mandela, King, and Gandhi all decry the way the human condition is hindered by the artificial distinctions we place between one another, like black/white, Christian/Muslim, man/woman, and gay/straight. We are all part of this thing called life, and it works best when we join together.

After more than forty years of trying to follow the great spiritual teacher Jesus of Nazareth, I have come to the conclusion that if my spirituality causes me to be elitist or feel superior to others in any way, then it is bogus. True spirituality is inclusive, not exclusive. You cannot find a single place in the four narratives of Jesus (the Gospels) where he refused to accept "the other"—not one. The tragedy is what has been done in his name since.

I do not mean to suggest that all religions are basically the same. There are legions of significant distinctions between the various faiths. But we must find a way to hold our beliefs passionately while exhibiting a humility that enables us to honor and learn from one another.

One way I try to remind myself of the importance of this serving others stuff is through a sign I keep posted on the inside of my office door at the hospital. It simply reads "Servant's Entrance." It is a gentle reminder of what it is I really want to do every time I leave my office to go onto the hospital floor.

GOING FOR THE GOLD

Among the many highlights of the 1964 Olympic Games in Tokyo was Billy Mills's performance in winning the ten-thousand-meter race. An Oglala Lakota Sioux from the very poor Pine Ridge Reservation in South Dakota, Mills came from behind to win, besting his own time by nearly fifty seconds, setting a world record, and becoming the only American ever to win the Olympic ten thousand meters.

I remember seeing an interview with Mills years later, when he was working on a Native American reservation teaching youth. He shared that until that moment when he was standing on the podium in Tokyo, he'd spent nearly all his life training to be an athlete. After winning the gold, he thought, *Now what? What do I do with the rest of my life?* During the playing of the U.S. national anthem after the race, as Mills stood there on the podium, he heard the voice of his late father speaking to him. He said, "Son, you can step out of the circle now. You can go on a journey to help others now, to empower others now."

Mills listened to that voice and has spent the remaining years of his life in service to Native American youth. The meaning of his life changed. He states, "I was constantly told and challenged to live my life as a warrior. As a warrior, you assume responsibility for yourself. The warrior humbles himself. And the warrior learns the power of giving."

Not only does life's meaning change with our circumstances, it is also deeply impacted by our familial and social roles. Most often, as Billy Mills discovered, the discovery of true meaning in life is involved in some way with helping others.

This paradoxical truth—that helping others is what really makes us happy—was brought home to me in a powerful way by my friend Brad. Recently Brad, who is not yet fifty, told our church family about what he'd learned from his own brush with death:

> As you know, I found myself in a bit of a pickle about three years ago when I was told that I had lymphoma. During the process of dealing with the disease, I spent much time thinking about my life. As I thought back, I appreciated how beautifully long my life has been. I was, and I am, thankful for so many incredible opportunities and experiences. I found that I didn't have, or want, a bucket list. I simply became extremely grateful for my life.
>
> And there was a pleasant surprise hidden in this. I looked at the times I had chosen to give; the time I spent rebuilding this building, the financial support that Julia and I have given to this church and other programs, and just the simple things I have done for others. Reflecting on this, I became a true fighter for my life. For me, the offerings that I had given to others truly gave my life value, and I became extremely thankful that I had not waited to act.
>
> For most of us, life has given us lots of time and lots of opportunities. We have had many days in which to choose our paths. I have learned that even though life is long and beautiful, there comes a day when each of our lives will get ex-

> tremely short. Suddenly, I found myself in a situation where I couldn't change the projection of my life. My strength was gone, and I didn't have tomorrow—in fact, not even that day—to do those things that I had put off. But it was in those moments that I found some of the strength I needed to fight for my life by reflecting on the actions I had taken in my past.
>
> Tomorrow is too late to do it today. For me, the giving of my time and our money to help others yesterday has literally helped give me a new lease on life today.

My friend Brad has discovered the true richness of living a meaningful life. Avoiding the distractions of our culture's fool's gold, he has discovered, through a harrowing experience, the true gold—what is real and what is lasting. His family and our little church community are all beneficiaries.

Jesus taught:

> Do not store up for yourselves treasures on earth, where moths and vermin destroy, and where thieves break in and steal. But store up for yourselves treasures in heaven, where moths and vermin do not destroy, and where thieves do not break in and steal. For where your treasure is, there your heart will be also. (Matthew 6:19–21 NIV)

Jesus teaches several important principles in this short passage. First, if we spend our lives acquiring this world's gold, we'll lose it one way or another. Either it will corrode or someone will just take it.

Second, he is saying that—while you can't take it with you—you can wire some ahead. Christian missionary Jim Elliot puts it like this, "He is no fool who gives what he cannot keep to gain what he cannot lose."[35] Elliot, Jesus, and my friend Brad are all challenging us to spend our time, our money, and our energy on things that will outlive us. That is, what we do for others.

Finally, Jesus notes that whatever we treasure will capture our hearts. Our hearts follow what we treasure. Therefore, choose wisely.

REMOVING THE CLUTTER

Among the many obstacles to choosing to live for others is the pressure applied by the religion of consumerism. Slogans like "The one who dies with the most toys wins" are sacred mantras for this particular brand of North American heresy. I've learned that the person who dies with the most toys still dies, and I've yet to meet anyone on his deathbed who wishes he had more stuff. All that matters in the end is being with loved ones, not loved things.

Katarina grew up in the picturesque mountains of Austria, but when I met her she was lying on a hospital bed in a cramped double room at an adult foster home. As I was getting to know Katarina, I asked her a question I don't ask nearly often enough, "What's one of the most important lessons you've learned in your seventy-plus years of living?" She didn't hesitate, "Simplify!"

When I asked her to unpack that instruction a little for me, Katarina spoke of how she'd had to liquidate nearly all of the possession she'd acquired during her lifetime when she moved into the foster home. In the process, she realized how unnecessary they really were. All that really mattered to her now was the love of her daughter, who visited her daily, and the simple joy they found in watching T*he Sound of Music* together on her daughter's computer. Katarina and her daughter both knew all the lines of the movie by heart, and they would laugh as they sang the familiar songs to each other like children.

This message to simplify was reinforced by Michael, whose deteriorating health made him a regular visitor to the hospital. On one particularly difficult admission, Michael was brought in to the ICU with a serious case of pneumonia and ended up on a ventilator. In the days that followed, while Michael was sedated and intubated, his wife of more than fifty years died. She'd been battling chronic obstructive pulmonary disease (COPD), a serious lung condition that diminishes airflow to the body. Michael's wife was found on the floor of their home by a neighbor who was checking in on her. Michael, lying in our ICU, had no idea that the woman he'd loved and cared for all these years was now dead. Since they had no children, we were all fretting over how and when to break the news to him after he was extubated.

I have to say, he actually did take the news quite well. "She was really sick, you know," he told me after being informed. But it was his choices afterward that really surprised me. Michael's brother came in from out of state to help make funeral plans for Michael's wife. While still recuperating in our ICU from his bout with pneumonia, Michael told his brother, "Go back to the house and get rid of everything you think I can live without. Sell it, throw it in a dumpster . . . I don't care. I just want at least 90 percent of the stuff gone."

Michael told me he wanted to "downsize" and buy a little cabin on the Rogue River where he could spend the summers with his brother like when they were kids. He and his brother had drifted apart over the years, and Michael felt that the recent turn of events, tragic as they were, offered an opportunity to reconnect with his only living family member. He wanted to make the most of it while he could.

The dying have repeatedly shown me that investing in relationships is wiser than striving for gold, which can disappear so quickly in a market downturn. I've also learned that the best evidence that one has led a meaningful life can be found in one's expressions of gratitude and generosity.

Evidence of a Grace-Filled Soul

■

The most important factor affecting our happiness is gratitude.

—DeWitt Jones, *For the Love of It*

NOT EVERYONE WANTS to see the hospice chaplain. I suppose some people fear the chaplain will try and force a deathbed conversion. Others may dread the guilt and shame that's often associated with clergy (and not without reason). And then, of course, there are those whose image of a chaplain is based on those awful portrayals from TV and the movies where the chaplain looks and acts like the Grim Reaper's stooge.

I'm fortunate. The nurses and social workers at my hospice work hard to allay the fears and concerns of both patients and their families about the dreaded call from the chaplain. In fact, our nurses enjoy teasing me about the fact that the patients who seem to enjoy my visits most are the atheists and agnostics. I'm still not sure what to make of that.

Still, I was somewhat surprised when a nurse told me that Abe had finally agreed to my offer to call on him for a get-to-know-you visit. I knew that Abe deeply loved his dearly departed wife Alma, his cheap beer, and his cigarettes—in that order. But I'd also been told Abe wanted nothing to do with religion. So I didn't expect he'd have any interest in speaking with me.

For the past few years, Abe's two surviving children had alternated staying with dad and taking care of him. They'd converted the back porch of the small weather-beaten frame house into a bedroom for Abe because Abe was a chain smoker and the kids couldn't take the smell.

When I arrived, he was sitting on a stool at his desk, clad in a stained undershirt and boxer shorts, finishing a bowl of cereal (it was around 1 P.M.), with a nearly finished cigarette dangling from his lower lip, and a small glass of beer for a chaser.

I had to yell several times that I was the chaplain because Abe was very hard of hearing.

He motioned for me to have a seat, looked me in the eye, and said, "I'm very glad you're here, because I'm really concerned about the hereafter. Every time I go into the kitchen, I say to myself, 'What am I here after?'" We laughed so hard his glass eye popped out—hence, I called him Popeye. Little, wiry, and with a gravelly voice worn out by ninety-two years of living, he sort of looked and sounded like Popeye, too.

We covered a lot of ground on that first visit. Abe told me he was born a Catholic but raised as a Baptist: "They sprinkled me as a baby and dunked me as a teenager—good waste of water both times." Abe's daughter told me later that Abe had been very religious before the war, and used to read his Bible every day, but he never went to church again after getting back from Europe. "He just couldn't get over all the killing and horror and both sides praying to God for victory."

Abe asked me if alcoholics went to hell.

"I dunno. Why?"

"My neighbor is a holy roller," Abe said, "and she told me that all alcoholics go to hell. I asked her what makes somebody an alcoholic, and she said, 'If you put all the beer and liquor someone consumed in their whole life together at one time and it's enough to make them drunk, then they'd go to straight to hell.' Guess I'm in deep shit."

"Me, too," I said. "See you there." We laughed again.

At the end of that visit, Abe said, "You can come back."

Over the months Abe and I developed a warm friendship. He took great delight in playfully trying to get me to admit that believing in God—any God—was foolish. For example, he pulled out the old theological conundrum, "If God can do anything, can He make a ball so heavy that He can't lift it?"

"I don't care," was my response.

"Comical," he replied.

This type of banter went on for several weeks. Then, one day he handed me the newsletter that came in the mail from our hospital. It contained the long list of donors who had contributed various amounts of money to the hospital over the years. Abe pointed out that he and his wife, Alma, were listed in the highest category of givers. Abe's daughter Shelly was there that day and told me about the donation Abe and Alma had made to the hospital ten years prior. It was an enormous amount of money.

I was stunned by both the incongruence and the generosity. Abe presented as a guy that didn't have two nickels to rub together. He lived on the back porch of a little frame house, drank the cheapest beer available, and bought only one pack of cigarettes at a time for fear that he'd die and leave some unsmoked.

He was watching my face intently as Shelly shared how much money Abe and Alma had donated. With deep sincerity, I looked

Abe in his good eye and thanked him for that contribution. I assured him that the money they'd given had helped a lot of people over the years, including myself—since I benefitted from having a job at the hospital. "Thank you so much," I blurted out through some gentle tears.

Abe really surprised me when he countered, "No, thank God." That was the only time Abe ever said the word "God" in a reverential way. Giving to others was the only act that my friend Abe considered to be holy.

Having heard that story, you may not be surprised to learn that there were many people at Abe's memorial service who spoke of how Abe had helped them out at some time of need in their lives, always in some unobtrusive way. Whether it was lending a hand to help a farmer get his crops in or providing a monetary "hand-out" in another's time of need, Abe had always been a neighbor others could count on.

For my money, that's evidence of a healthy soul.

THE TRAIN WRECK

Regardless of one's religious affiliation or protestations of assurance of salvation, I have discovered that gratitude is the surest sign of contented heart. Real gratitude is hard to fake. It wells up from the inside and graces everyone and everything around it.

Earlier I quoted Henri Nouwen, who called dying "the most important act of living" because it offers us a choice between binding the people we love with guilt or setting them free in gratitude.[36] My patient Betty was a vivid portrayal of Nouwen's insight.

Betty was reluctant to see me, but her nurse had talked her into it. Even though Betty was sad and depressed, she was reluctant to speak with a chaplain, because she'd never been big on religion.

When I met her, she was seated on her hospital bed in her living room, breathing with the aid of oxygen. The tube running from the electric concentrator delivered the needed oxygen into Betty's nostrils with the ever-present whoosh-whoosh sound. Betty found the sound annoying.

Betty was not a happy person. She'd been married five times, and each of her five children had a different dad. Her one joy in life, shopping, was a distant memory now that she was nearly bedridden. The bedside commode gave evidence of her most recent indignity.

As she was complaining about how rarely her children came to see her, the phone rang. It was a daughter from California. Because of hearing loss, Betty had the phone turned up as loud as it could go, so I was able to hear the whole three-minute conversation.

Betty's daughter began by apologizing that she wouldn't be able to drive up today for her planned visit because she'd had an out-of-the-blue job interview. She'd been unable to find work for more than four years. But this interview came up suddenly, she went, and she actually got the job. It was in a hospital and the pay was more than $18 an hour plus benefits. The daughter was ecstatic. Her excitement was jumping through the telephone.

After a short pause, Betty glumly replied, "Well, I hope I'm still alive when you get here."

It was like watching a train wreck and being unable to stop it.

At least four times in the brief conversation I heard Betty's daughter desperately and joyously share "I got the job!" Someone wanted her. Someone saw something hirable in her. And she had phoned her mother aching to hear similar words of acceptance. But none came.

Betty was so imprisoned by her own pains and need for acceptance that she had nothing to give her daughter.

It was a tragic scene.

I wanted to grab the phone and shout, "Congratulations! You're spectacular! They're lucky to get you. Get here when you can and drive safely, but I'm so proud of you!" But I didn't.

Now, I don't know what misery Betty had endured that robbed her of the ability to give the gift of acceptance to a daughter who desperately wanted to hear she was special. Betty never told me. But I do want to learn from Betty's pain.

I want to cultivate the wonder of gratitude in my life so that I can offer as much loving acceptance to others as I can. I realize, however, my intentions aren't simply that pure and noble. There is a part of me that knows one day when I find myself bedridden with oxygen tubes shoved up my nose, I don't want to be sad and alone.

HOMER' S ODYSSEY

> Clarksburg, WV—Homer J. Carmichael, 74, a prominent local businessman, died Sunday, November 5, 2000, in his home at Lake Floyd, following a long history of heart problems. Known to all as "Hoagy," he was born December 12, 1926, in Clarksburg.

Although nearly twenty-five years my senior, Hoagy was one of my best friends. We met when I was in my early thirties. I was working in Wheeling at a small advertising agency owned by my father. Hoagy was the managing partner for the Sheraton Hotel in Clarksburg, and we were their ad guys. Actually, the Sheraton was one of my dad's accounts. But after working on a small project with me, Hoagy (not so politely) asked my dad to stay in Wheeling and have me make the two-hour drive down to Clarksburg for the monthly meetings. This pissed my dad off—but won my heart. When Hoagy and I were together, we were like little kids. We just clicked.

As time moved along, I lost touch with Hoagy. Nearly ten years later, when I was pastor of a small church in Melbourne, Florida, Hoagy and I reconnected. He had sold his share in the hotel and just happened to retire in Melbourne.

As I've mentioned before, Maya Angelou once said, "I've learned that people will forget what you said, people will forget what you did, but people will never forget how you made them feel." Hoagy made me feel like a little kid again. Hoagy reminded me how to play.

Hoagy had known his share of grief. One of his sons, a local football hero, died tragically in his teenage years. His beloved wife had died of cancer. When we reconnected, he and his second wife were going through a divorce. During the divorce, Hoagy moved in with our family until things got sorted out. I can still remember hearing him trundle into our kitchen at 3 A.M. after getting up to pee. He'd go to the refrigerator, take out the orange juice (with the pulp in it), shake the carton three times, and pour himself a drink before going back to bed. Every morning I'd complain that he woke me up again, and he'd just laugh.

Hoagy was not big on church—in other words, he never went. So I was surprised when he asked if he could come along when I was invited to preach at a small church on the other side of Orlando.

During the sermon, I told one of my favorite stories about an Indian boy. As I learned it, this particular tribe of First Peoples had a specific ritual to mark the passage of a boy's coming into manhood. When a young boy arrived at the age of thirteen, his father would take him into the deepest, darkest part of the forest. The boy had to spend the night alone in the woods with only his small tomahawk for protection. In the morning, if the boy survived, he would be welcomed back to the tribe, no longer as a young boy but as a brave.

According to the story, one young boy was taken by his father into the forest around sunset. His father kissed him, said the appropriate blessings, and left. The boy was alone. All night.

He couldn't fall asleep for fear. Every snap of a twig or hoot of an owl frightened him. He was tormented by thoughts of a hungry cougar or bear catching his scent and tearing him to pieces. His little fists had a death grip on that small tomahawk.

The night seemed to go on forever. For hours he kept his eyes on the distant mountains in the east, knowing the sun would rise beyond them to announce the morning when he would no longer be a little boy but now a brave.

He waited and waited until, at last, the awful black of the far eastern sky began to turn purple, then a glimmer of orange, and finally the bright yellow of the sun began to poke its head up for his first day of manhood. His heart was pounding with relief and excitement until he noticed a dark shadow behind a large pine tree about fifty yards away. The little boy thought the worst. "Have I endured this long awful night only to be eaten by a grizzly bear just before my father arrives to take me home?"

But as the sun moved up, the shadow diminished and he could see that it wasn't a grizzly bear after all. It was his father! And his father had his large bow for hunting. When his father emerged with great pride from behind the pine, he told his son that the custom of their people was for the father to stay with the son all night long to provide protection in case of danger.

After the appropriate blessings were chanted, father and son began the journey home to celebrate the tribe's newest brave. As they walked, the little boy thought to himself, "How foolish I was! If I'd have known my father was there, I wouldn't have been afraid at all, and I could have enjoyed a beautiful night in the forest."

Just because we can't see the being we name God doesn't mean God's not here with us right now, watching over us and protecting us in whatever dark we find ourselves in. For God has said, "I will not in any way fail you nor give you up nor leave you without support. I will not, I will not, I will not in any degree leave you helpless nor forsake nor let you down, nor relax My hold on you! Assuredly not!" (Hebrews 13:5 AMP)

As we drove home, with tears in his eyes Hoagy told me, "That little Indian boy story . . . Grewe, you really got me with that one. Grewe, you're the best preacher I've ever heard."

I said, "Hoagy, since you've only been to church ten times in your whole life, I don't think I'd call that a ringing endorsement." Again, we just laughed and cried together.

Time passed and we'd moved to St. Louis while Hoagy moved back to Clarksburg, West Virginia—but we stayed in touch. Several summers later, Hoagy had a heart attack and ended up in the Clarksburg hospital. I drove the ten hours from St. Louis just to spend July 4th with him. We spent the whole day together in his hospital room. It was the last time I saw him alive. I can't remember much of anything we talked about—but I do know he tearfully reminded about the little Indian boy story. He always did.

What I do remember is how grateful he was for his life, for his son Brad, and for his grandkids. Looking back, in all the years I knew Hoagy, I never heard him complain. I think that's why I drove ten hours just to see him. Gratitude is magnetic. It's attractive. Hoagy's gratitude was always a refreshing tonic in a world terrified by the fear of not enough, and I wanted as much as I could get.

The Sting of the Scorpion

■

Thank God, thank God that I am like other men,

that I am only a man among others.

—Thomas Merton, *Conjectures of a Guilty Bystander*

I WISH I COULD TELL YOU I love every person I visit. Fact is, there are some folks I meet in this work whom I just don't like.

For instance, I remember Phyllis. Phyllis was some sort of insurance salesperson who, upon learning of her inoperable pancreatic cancer, had her son drive her to a party some friends were having so she could share her personal drama and be the center of attention. With more than $50,000 in credit card debt that would never be repaid and her home and car in the process of being repossessed, Phyllis acted like someone who'd just hit the lottery. "No bank will foreclose on someone who's dying," she gleefully told me. Old lovers showed up to treat her to fancy dinners. Local churches and service clubs invited her to speak on how she could be so courageous in the face of such a prognosis. Phyllis acted like it was one grand party in her honor, and she wouldn't have to pay the bill. As you can tell, she really got under my skin.

Brian and his partner, Becky, annoyed me, too. They had hooked up while each of them was still married to someone else. Both were obese, bigoted, and incredibly mean to their children. Every time I left their home, I thanked God I was just a chaplain and not a family therapist or social worker.

And then there are those whose lives have been stolen by drug or alcohol addictions. Sheila had attractive streaks of silver highlighting her long raven black hair. But slimy stumps had replaced her once-white teeth due to years of using crystal meth. Her brain was mush, and her emaciated tiny body had dozens of stage-four wounds from years of neglect and drug abuse.

The nursing home in which Sheila now lived left the TV in her room on the Cartoon Network 24/7 because Sheila, age fifty-five, liked cartoons. When I first met her, I noticed on the tray table next to her bed three very large Cheetos cheese twists, a Pop Tart with one bite taken out of it, and an open can of Ensure—unusual diet choices for a woman who couldn't have weighed eighty pounds soaking wet.

Sheila told me she loved Jesus and loved her church, although she couldn't remember the name of her church or her pastor. In my work as a chaplain, this is pretty common fare. Folks tend to tell the preacher what they think she or he wants to hear. It comes with the territory.

Additionally, I encounter patients whose experiences simply unnerve me. Addicts and Alzheimer's patients are the most painful for me. It's hard to watch the bodies of these once vibrant human beings deteriorate even after their minds and souls have already been stolen by drugs or disease. Deep down I think I'm afraid of both—drugs and dementia.

This fear was really brought home to me after I'd spent an hour with Thomas. As I drove away from the shit hole of a house that Thomas, his wife, and their two young children called home, I was angry. Not at Thomas—but at the drugs that had hijacked his life.

Being with Thomas was like being with Gollum from *The Lord of the Rings.* A tiny little man whose brain had been rotted out by years of smoking pot, Thomas spent his days sitting in his recliner and talking to himself, oblivious to the cancer that was eating his body alive. A large picture of his father, who'd been a police officer, was hanging over Thomas's bed. Thomas also had a large collection of superhero dolls—Batman, Superman, the Green Lantern, and the like—on display in his room. He told me they were "action figures, not dolls" and "collectables." Then, with this weird little laugh, he said to himself, "But he won't understand, will he?" Thomas had once been a talented musician with dreams of becoming a rock star. But now here he sat, stoned and dying.

Now, I realize the struggles I've had with these people and others I've met are my issues. I don't know the pains or disappointments or life situations that had a hand in forming who these folks became. I was only privy to the end of their stories. But these tortured souls have forced me to face some of my own demons. What ugliness resides in me? How do I anesthetize my own pain? Can I offer the grace of loving acceptance even to people I don't like? Can I extend care to people who repulse me? Or am I just another ordained bullshit artist?

LEARNING COMPASSION

The wonderful Henri Nouwen reframed an old story that has been a great help to me on my own journey to discover the grace of compassion.

> Once there was a very old man who used to mediate early every morning under a large tree on the bank of the Ganges

> River in India. One morning, having finished meditation, the old man opened his eyes and saw a scorpion floating hopelessly in the strong current of the river. As the scorpion was pulled close to the tree, it got caught in the long tree roots that branched out far into the river. The scorpion struggled frantically to free itself but got more and more entangled in the complex network of tree roots.
>
> When the old man saw this, he immediately stretched himself onto the extended roots and reached out to rescue the drowning scorpion. But as soon as he touched it, the animal jerked and stung him wildly. Instinctively, the man withdrew his hand, but then, after having regained his balance, he once again stretched himself out along the roots to save the agonized scorpion. But every time the old man came within reach, the scorpion stung him so badly with its poisonous tail that his hands became swollen and bloody and his face distorted in pain.
>
> At that moment, a passerby saw the old man stretched out on the roots struggling with the scorpion and shouted: "Hey, stupid old man. What's wrong with you? Only a fool risks his life for the sake of an ugly, useless creature. Don't you know that you may kill yourself to save that ungrateful animal?"
>
> Slowly the old man turned his head and, looking calmly in the stranger's eyes, he said, "Friend, because it is the nature of the scorpion to sting, why should I give up my own nature to save?"
>
> Well, that's the question: Why should we give up our nature to be compassionate even when we get stung in a biting, stinging world?[37]

This is the real question: *Can I be a compassionate human being while living in a world that bites and stings?*

At this point in my life, being a compassionate human is my main goal. And why is compassion such a big deal to me? Because that's how the Mystery we name God has always dealt with me. I feel it is my duty and my joy to pass it along.

When you think of God, what is the first word that comes to your mind? Holy? Judge? Fear? For me, the first word is *compassionate.* Where do I get this? From the Bible—in particular, from the book of Exodus.

In Exodus, this Being we name God is incredibly mysterious. First, God's entrance is quite dramatic, interrupting Moses's day by appearing in the form of a burning bush that is mysteriously not consumed. After numerous adventures together, God and Moses find themselves on a mountaintop (Sinai) in the middle of a desert. At this point in the story, Moses makes a surprising request. He wants to know God's name.

In the biblical era, names were very important. To know someone's name was a sign of having power over him or her. That's why God often gave a person a new name—it was a sign of special relationship.

So in a highly unusual twist, Moses asks to learn God's real name. It's a bold request, perhaps an impertinent one. Yet God does not deny it. In one of the most intimate scenes of the Hebrew Scriptures, God hides Moses in the cleft of a rock, passes in front of him (letting Moses view God's "hinder parts") and God declares God's own name to Moses. Now this isn't some journalist describing God's name—this is God's Self declaring God's name.

"And God passed in front of Moses, proclaiming, 'The Lord, the Lord, the *compassionate* and gracious God . . .'" (Exodus 34:6 NIV [italics mine]). The first adjective that God uses to describe God's Self is compassion. Of all the things God could have said—holy, omnipotent (all-powerful), omniscient (all-knowing), omnipresent (everywhere all the time), handsome (good looking)

—God chooses compassionate. This is very telling. Our English word "compassion" is a compound word. The prefix *com* means "along with" and the root, *passio*, is from the Latin, meaning "to suffer." God is declaring to Moses and to us, "I am the God who suffers with you."

Now, if I'd been there instead of Moses, I might have popped off with something like, "God, I think it's great that You want to suffer with us . . . but is there Somebody else up there? Someone who can keep suffering *away* from us? I'd prefer it if suffering never came near my tent."

But that's not the God we have, according to the Bible. The God of the Scriptures is a God who has chosen to suffer with us. If you think this is crazy talk, how else do you explain the crucifixion? The core of the Christian message is that God loves us so much that God became one of us and chose to die rather than live without us. Further, our faith proclaims that this mysterious God will never leave us.

So back to the central question, the scorpion question: How can I be a conduit of grace for those folks I don't like or who make me afraid?

The Buddhist Thich Nhat Hanh teaches a simple chant I find quite helpful. "Feelings come and go like clouds in a windy sky."[38] This reminds me that my feelings of uneasiness, judgment, and possibly even loathing are just like clouds on a windy day. They come, and they go. I don't have to be ruled by these fickle, fleeting clouds of feeling. I can choose to behave in ways that are loving and accepting toward those entrusted to my care, even if I don't feel like it. In this way I can honor both my understanding of God and my intentional goal of being a compassionate human.

I don't know the whole story of any of the people I meet. I don't know all the sorrows and life situations that helped form them. Each of the individuals I encounter in my work is a mystery—as we all are. And significantly, it is not in my job description (or my power) to change anyone. All I can do is seek to behave in a grace-filled manner, trusting that God's amazing awful grace will supply whatever is needed for both of us in each moment.

At the heart of my struggle with folks like Phyllis or Thomas or Brian or Sheila is the illusion that I am different from or superior to them. I have created a scenario in my mind where I am not like "them." I have made them "other"—and whenever we demonize the "other," we can no longer learn from them. Spiritual heroes like Gandhi, King, Mandela, and Merton all are adamant on this point. The reality is that the people I work with each day are all my sisters and my brothers. We are all in this life together.

Truth be told, I still find there are some folks for whom I just don't have it to give. I'm not able to extend to every person the kind of grace-filled care I feel every person should receive. In those cases, I rely on the built-in genius of the hospice program. I am simply one member of a team. Our program includes nurses, social workers, home health aides, and volunteers, all of whom help provide loving care, spiritual nurture, and compassionate support. I'm grateful to be part of such a team because, as I have come to learn, on any given day, the scorpion might be me.

Letting Go

■

Leaden blankets weigh her down,
White hanks drape her leathery face.
Caught in the numbness of narrowing time,
Eyes blinded by gauze,
Robotic signs echo into her coma.
Metallic hiss of breathing machine is the
Strange violence of modern compassion.

—Deng Ming-Dao[39]

This letting go stuff is hard. Really hard.

When I first met Sophia, she was thrashing around on the bed in her hospital room. A friend told me she'd been a spiritual teacher for years. But now she was dying. At four-foot-something, she looked like a little elf. As I sat holding her hand for more than an hour, she came in and out of consciousness. In her more lucid moments, she taught me the three core principles of her teaching: (1) give loving allowance to those who think differently than you do; (2) give greater communication to what you truly believe; and (3) take responsibility for your own emotional health. She told me these principles had been given to her directly from "the Other Side—what you would call heaven." I knew this little woman with the twinkle in her eye had something to teach me, and I prayed we'd have enough time together for me to learn it.

Sophia did recover from whatever had caused her hospitalization and was discharged home to our hospice service. It was my joy and privilege to really get to know this fascinating woman. I learned that Sophia's father had been a Methodist minister. Sophia idolized her dad; her mother, not so much. She really hadn't liked her mother and was troubled by those parts of herself that she saw as reflections of her mother's character. Sophia had only one child, a daughter, from whom she was emotionally estranged. Sophia's daughter was a born again Christian whose goal was to get Sophia saved—a goal Sophia did not share.

Sophia, mind you, was a true spiritual mentor to many people, both locally and around the country. She referred to God as "the Cosmos," and they (Sophia and "the Cosmos") were in direct communication. When I asked Sophia what she thought about the prospect of death, she responded with glee, stating, "Oh, you mean the joyous transition of leaving my body? I can't think of anything more wonderful."

Sophia's "joyous transition" took much longer than she, I, or the hospice team ever imagined.

As the days turned into weeks, and the weeks turned into months, I visited with Sophia regularly at her beautiful little apartment in an assisted living complex. During that time, Sophia struggled mightily with the ongoing loss of both her autonomy and her meaning. These two titanic losses are the cause of most of the spiritual pain I encounter as a hospice chaplain.

The loss of autonomy has several key stages that I have witnessed firsthand. The first is when a patient loses the ability to drive a car. The thought of no longer being able to go where you want when you want is a major blow to the North American ego and unleashes for many the horrifying dread of becoming increasingly dependent on others. In other words, becoming "a burden." The resulting emotional havoc can be quite paralyzing.

The next incremental loss is often the ability to walk without the aid of assistance—be it a cane, a walker, or a wheelchair.

For some folks, there is also the loss of memory. As the various forms of dementia attack once vibrant minds, feelings of vulnerability and confusion create tremendous fear. Where am I? Who am I? Whom can I trust? Am I safe?

Then comes the final indignity, when a hospital bed gets placed in the living room and one loses the ability even to get up to go to the toilet. This loss is often accompanied by the physically painful insertion of a catheter.

All these losses, and others along the way, come with their own pain and attendant grieving. Most folks are unable to take them in stride. They really hurt.

When you couple these losses of autonomy with a loss of meaning, spiritual suffering is the result. Sophia experienced this suffering with great dignity and grace.

At the beginning of our relationship, Sophia was busy with visits from friends and phone calls and e-mails from followers around the country. But as the months wore on, those dwindled down, and Sophia often sat all alone in her apartment watching the busy traffic run up and down I-5. The traffic was a constant reminder to Sophia that younger and more vibrant people had places to go and things to do—but she did not. She was alone. Alone and unneeded. It was during this time that the Cosmos began to speak to her about "dissolution."

I remember she asked me to look up the word for her in a dictionary. "Dissolution" means the breaking of a bond, tie, union, or partnership. Sophia was experiencing the *dissolution* of her soul, her mind, and her body. Her body was decaying, her memories were becoming progressively lost, and her soul ached to be released into the joyous transition of the Cosmos.

One day as we were talking about her experience of dissolution, we began to explore the importance many faith traditions place on the ability to surrender. Surrendering to reality. Accepting things as they really are, not as we wish they were.

So much of our existential pain is caused by this inability to accept reality, particularly the supreme reality that we are not the center of the universe. Our egos, no matter how developed they are, cling to being the center of life and are not easily displaced; yet, paradoxically, we will not find true happiness until the ego is overcome.

During my conversation with this beautifully wise woman, I wondered if this might be what Jesus was talking about when he said, "Blessed are the poor in spirit, for theirs is the kingdom of heaven" (Matthew 5:3). The poor have had a lifetime of experience forcing them to surrender their egos. The poor know firsthand what it is to be dependent on others. The poor tend to be profoundly aware that they are not independent beings. The surrender that death requires as a prerequisite to entering heaven's gates is nothing new to those who have been forced to surrender simply to survive.

Not so for the rich. Looking back over the years of my chaplaincy, I've found that the rich often have a much more difficult time coping with the indignities that dying demands. Sophia was not wealthy financially, but she was rich in the esteem she enjoyed from others for so many years. As we often discussed, this loss of status caused her a great deal of soul suffering. "How hard it is for the rich to enter the kingdom of God," Jesus was also known to say (Mark 10:23 NIV).

As we spoke that afternoon in her apartment, I wondered why surrendering seems to be the last great lesson death has to teach most of us. Is it because we will need to know how to surrender as we move into whatever comes next?

As it turned out, Sophia would have to endure even more "dissolution" before her joyous transition. Because she was not dying quickly enough to appease the government (for fear of wasting Medicare dollars), we had to discharge Sophia from our hospice service. Now, at first blush, you might think being discharged from hospice is good news. Not so. Folks who have received the wonderful care of a hospice team often feel emotionally set adrift after being discharged. No more nurses visiting several times a week. No more home health aides to provide baths and personal hygiene care. No more volunteers coming to read or share stories. No more delivery of needed medications to the front door. And worst of all, no more visits from incredibly good-looking and insightful chaplains.

Perhaps the greatest indignity was when Sophia was forced to move out of her cute little apartment, with all her cherished mementoes from a life well lived, and relocate to a skilled nursing facility. Sophia's last days were spent in a room with two other bed-ridden residents in a hot, stale, urine-smelling nursing home.

But Sophia thrived in her new environment. All the years she'd invested in her practice of spirituality paid off at the end. Sophia somehow learned by *the awful grace of God* to surrender to her fate, and she found meaning in helping cheer up not only her roommates but also those who worked in the nursing home. I can honestly say that she was radiant the last time I saw her.

On that last visit, she was particularly excited because her brother Arthur was present. (Now, Arthur had been dead for many years.) Sophia was sure the Cosmos had sent Arthur to help usher her into her joyous transition. Seems she was right after all.

WHO DETERMINES WHAT *A GOOD DEATH* IS?

This "letting go" stuff is hard. How do you even know what to fight and what to surrender to? Many of the patients I see are ready to die. They're in their eighties or nineties, they've led full lives, and they're simply ready to get on with it.

But others are not ready for death. They love their lives and their families, and they still have unfulfilled hopes and dreams. How can they simply accept their disease and give up? Often, the teaching of the so-called experts makes these patients feel guilty for not wanting to surrender to death. They want to fight. So I encourage them to. They ask me to pray for their healing, and I do.

As I write these words, my dear friend and teacher Peg is fighting for her life. Peg is in her late fifties and has been battling for more than four years the ALS (amyotrophic lateral sclerosis, or Lou Gehrig's disease) that steals more of her breath and muscle strength each day. Folks with slowly debilitating diseases like ALS and Parkinson's have learned to survive by battling the disease, so finding the "off" switch that would allow them to just give in and surrender is really hard. Peg knows her existential pain would be alleviated somewhat if she could surrender to her disease process, but it's not that simple. Time and time again, she has implored me, "How do I do it?"

The dying person must also contend with his or her own survival biology. As Peg struggles for each breath, the reptilian part of her brain kicks into overdrive, flooding her withering body with adrenaline and overriding her rational thoughts about the need to let go with its fight to stay alive. How do you simply surrender in such a difficult situation?

Or what about those folks who love their families and love life so much they just don't want to go yet? I remember Theresa, who couldn't have weighed more than seventy pounds. She couldn't sleep and was visibly in pain, but she was really upset when her daughter, Samantha, told her it was okay to die. Samantha had read that it is a good idea to tell a loved one who is near death that he or she is free to go. It can be a beautiful gift to release the loved one so he or she will die in peace, the author proclaimed.

Often, this is true. But not always.

My friend Petey taught me this lesson. We'd been praying for a miracle healing for about three years, when he suddenly began to decline physically. Concerned that he had very little time left, I asked him if he'd taken care of all the financial things necessary for his family's welfare. Petey got really angry and screamed, "You're killing my faith!" About three hours later, he called to apologize and told me he'd taken care of everything. He died within the week.

Nowadays, I often say to folks, "Look, the doctors and the nurses have important degrees, lots of letters after their names, and stethoscopes and test results and other powerful tools that give them some idea of what is happening with you. But you're the one living inside your body, and I think you know best. You know what it's like in there. You'll know when things are changing. Trust your own heart."

So many of the family members and friends I meet talk about wanting to help their loved one have "a good death." I'm uncomfortable with that phrase. I think it's patronizing. Who determines what "a good death" is? And how is this measured? I find it more helpful to think in terms of helping patients have "a better death." By that, I mean the individual experiences a better death than if the hospice team were not present. I believe patients should determine for themselves what constitutes "a good death." It's not my call. My hope is that each person I visit feels a little better while I'm there or after I leave than before I arrived.

QUIT YOUR BITCHIN'

Margaret was a devout Presbyterian, ninety-five-year-old bedbound lady whose loving family had nicknamed her "Bulldog." Barely five foot and maybe a hundred pounds soaking wet, this little spitfire of a woman had helped guide and shape her family for four generations. She was deeply loved and cared for by her offspring.

I wasn't in her home five minutes when she started badgering me, "Why am I still here? Why won't God take me? I'm ready to die . . . I've lived a wonderful life and I'm ready to go. What's taking God so long?"

I looked her right in the eye and told her, "Look, I've been a minister for more than forty years and if there's one thing I've learned, it's this—God is horrible . . ." She was stunned and I had her full attention, "God is horrible," I said, "*at taking orders.*" She laughed hard. I continued, "Margaret, I've tried to teach God how to take orders. I really have. I've screamed, and yelled, and threatened—it just doesn't work. God shows no interest to learn."

We became instant friends.

That little conversation helped alleviate her existential pain for a little while. But when I returned the following week it was back.

"I'm ready to go. Why won't God take me? I hate just laying here and waiting . . ." Margaret complained.

"Look, you're dying," I replied. "But you're not in pain, you're in a comfortable bed, you're safe and warm, and the people who love you most are caring for you. At this time of life it just doesn't get any better than this. Quit your bitchin'."

"Thanks," she said and then laughingly, "I needed that." Margaret was a bulldog after all.

When Death nears it shatters the illusion that we are somehow in control of our lives. Dying can liberate us by enabling us to see life as it really is, and living in reality is heroic living. As I've said, living in reality is where we are likely to encounter God. But sometimes reality can just plain be a scary place.

WRESTLING WITH GOD KNOWS WHAT?

Genesis 32 contains an archetypal story about the human condition. The main character is the third Jewish patriarch, Jacob. Jacob was born immediately after his twin brother, Esau. As he came from the womb, Jacob was clutching his older brother's heel, as if to pull him back so Jacob could be born first. As we know all too well, second-place finishers don't get the gold medal. In that culture, being the firstborn son was like hitting the lottery. When it came time for the inheritances to be doled out, the firstborn son would get twice as much (the double portion) as the other sons (girls were generally left out altogether).

The name Jacob means "supplanter" or, in our vernacular, "little thief," and the biblical Jacob surely lived up to his name. First, he conned his older brother out of his birthright. (Esau was a big strong guy but apparently not the sharpest knife in the drawer.) Then Jacob and his mother schemed to steal Esau's blessing from their dying father. This later incident so infuriated the hotheaded Esau that Jacob literally had to run for his life. While Jacob was staying with some out-of-town relatives and allowing the situation at home to cool off, his conniving nature surfaced again in his dealings with Uncle Laban (a pretty good con man in his own right).

Jacob fell in love with Laban's daughter Rachel and worked seven years for the right to marry her. But on their wedding night Laban pulled the old switcheroo. Jacob woke up the next morning married to Leah, Rachel's older and less attractive sister. Jacob worked another seven years to wed the woman he loved. But during that time, he also ripped off Uncle Laban and became a very wealthy man. This did not sit well with the in-laws. So, in the middle of the night, Jacob took his wives, his kids, his livestock—all his stuff—and split. This is all really in the Bible, I swear.

As Jacob is heading back home, he gets word that big brother Esau is coming out to meet him with an army of four hundred men. Jacob is stuck. He has nowhere to run. It's time for the "little thief" to face his demons. Jacob discovers, as we all do at some point, that you can only outrun your flawed nature for so long. Call it karma, come-uppance, or chickens coming home to roost, but we can't hide from our woundedness forever.

On the night before the big showdown, Jacob and his family are safely ensconced on the other side of the river Jabbok. If Esau attacks, Jacob figures his family can make a run for it while Esau and his men are crossing the water). In that moment, all Jacob's past conniving seems to have caught up with him. It's into this dramatic scene that the sacred author now inserts the quintessential *Deus ex machina.* God shows up—unexpected, uninvited, and inhospitable —and attacks Jacob. Actually, the text says they wrestle, but there is nothing to indicate this is horseplay. This is an all-night fight to the death.

As morning brings the sun, God orders Jacob to let him go. (Actually, the Hebrew text refers to this supernatural wrestler alternately as a man, an angel, and God. Perhaps the sacred author was as confused as we are by this interlude.) When Jacob refuses to release him, God pulls a fast one and wrenches Jacob's hip out of joint. Before God disappears into the night, God blesses Jacob and changes his name to Israel.

So what's this hauntingly crazy story about? What do we do with a God who attacks us when we're down?

As I read it, this story is about Jacob confronting his own wounded soul and, in the process, being healed by *the awful grace of God*.

My basis for understanding the story this way lies in the renaming of Jacob. Name is an important biblical concept; it encompasses the whole of personhood. God's renaming Jacob is illustrative of God changing Jacob's basic character. He is no longer "little thief," but becomes Israel, which is translated here as "he who wrestles with God" and elsewhere in the Hebrew Scriptures as "prince of God." In this enigmatic interlude, Jacob's past catches up to him. Through a long soul-searching night, *the awful grace of God* comes and painfully liberates Jacob from his own conniving false self. Interestingly, the evidence of this liberation is that Jacob/Israel walks with a limp for the rest of his life. Joan Chittister notes that Jacob "walks into the struggle but he limps out of it, permanently marked, forever changed."[40]

And what is the pivotal point to Jacob's receiving this blessing? He surrenders. Chittister writes:

> Exhaustion is the invisible enemy, the real enemy, in struggle. It's when we won't let go of a thing that we are defeated by it. "Let me go . . . ," says the Spirit of God. And Jacob answers, "I will not let you go until you bless me." And therein lies the secret of winning all the struggles of our lives. We must learn to let go of them so that we can come to the blessings hidden within them.[41]

The paradox is that even though Jacob never quit struggling, he knew when to let go.

WE'LL SEE

Nettie was bored to death. She used to love reading books and doing crossword puzzles, but as her eyesight diminished, so did her quality of life. A lovely woman living in a small apartment that she kept at 85 degrees. Whenever I visited her, she always had on full makeup and a dress. Nettie was a lady—and always had been. Think June Cleaver without the pearls.

A devout Christian with a Methodist background, Nettie was ready to die—and the waiting around with nothing to do was getting on her nerves. She was also bothered by the ever-increasing loss of autonomy. She loved my visits because they were a distraction from her terminal boredom and her slow but steady physical decline.

Nettie liked to talk about her experiences of growing up in the Sams Valley of southern Oregon. She told me about her neighbor, the "Yoo-Hoo Girl," who got that name because she used to run out to the road yelling "Yoo-Hoo" whenever boys would drive by. Nettie's parents forbade her from taking part in that kind of activity so as not to get a reputation.

We laughed a lot during our visits. But most of all Nettie wanted me to tell her stories. She had made her peace with God, thought about her own death quite a bit, and simply wanted a vacation from it all. That's where I came in. I was a distraction.

I remember her favorite story was a Taoist story I like to tell about a Chinese farmer.

> A man who lived on the northern frontier of China was skilled in interpreting events. One day, for no reason, his horse ran away to the nomads across the border. Everyone tried to console him, but his father said, "We'll see."
>
> Some months later his horse returned, bringing a splendid nomad stallion. Everyone congratulated him, but his father said, "We'll see."
>
> Their household was richer by a fine horse, which his son loved to ride. One day his son fell and broke his hip. Everyone tried to console him, but his father said, "We'll see."

> A year later the nomads came in force across the border, and every able-bodied man took his bow and went into battle. The Chinese frontiersmen lost nine of every ten men. Only because the son was lame did the father and son survive to take care of each other.

That Taoist tale became a source of relief for Nettie from the debilitation of self-pity. As she continued to lose her physical capacities, the story of the Chinese farmer became a game. For example, when she told me about the indignity of no longer being able to urinate without the aid of a catheter, I tried to console her. A girlish smile emerged from her face when she replied, "We'll see."

On my last visit she was lying on her hospital bed, no longer able to get up, and barely able to talk. When I said goodbye and told her I'd miss her, she was able to wink and say, "We'll see."

Whole Lotta Shakin' Going On

Our medical system is excellent at trying to stave off death with $8,000-a-month chemotherapy, $3,000-a-day intensive care, $5,000-an-hour surgery. But, ultimately, death comes, and no one is good at knowing when to stop.

—Atul Gawande, "Letting Go," *The New Yorker*

As part of my training for chaplaincy, I spent a year in residency doing clinical pastoral education (CPE) at a teaching hospital in St. Louis. CPE is the basic form of instruction for would-be chaplains and involves working twenty to forty hours per week while also taking about eight hours a week of instruction, personal counseling, and group therapy. Many seminary students take one three-month unit of CPE. Board-certified chaplains must complete at least four units, and many chaplains take more. I completed five units.

The schedule during my residency year was brutal. I worked as a hospital chaplain on Monday, Tuesday, and Wednesday from 8:00 A.M. to 4:30 P.M., and then on Thursdays from 8:00 A.M. until 7:00

the next morning—twenty-three hours in a row. From 5:00 P.M. on Thursday evening until the next morning, I was the only chaplain in our 250-bed, Level 1 Trauma Center—which meant I was up all night answering emergency calls.

I learned a lot about myself that year. I discovered that I'm an adrenaline junkie, that I'm wired to be a calming influence in the midst of drama and chaos, and that I find great meaning in working to be an agent of grace during particularly painful experiences.

During my residency year, I really enjoyed the opportunities I had to teach. I remember one particular on-call Thursday night when a new CPE student arrived to shadow me. I was expected to show my new trainee, Amy, around the hospital, give her the lay of the land, and explain what the on-call chaplain does. When Amy introduced herself to me, she was wide-eyed, eager, and scared to death.

Shortly after we completed our tour of the hospital, my pager went off for a call on the eighth-floor ICU. The eighth floor was my regular area of service, so I had a pretty good sense of the patients and families and what was going on there.

We were called to Mr. Jenkins's room. Mr. Jenkins was in his mid-sixties and had been intubated and sedated for more than three days. He hadn't moved a muscle during that time. His family had been holding vigil throughout those days and had just made the gut-wrenching decision to "withdraw care." I hate that phrase. "Withdraw care" is hospital code language for taking a patient off of a ventilator and/or feeding tube and letting nature take its course—which leads most often to death. But the reality is that the hospital never stops caring for the patient; they just shift gears and provide a different kind of care. The staff does everything possible to alleviate suffering so the patient can die without needlessly prolonging the pain.

Mr. Jenkins's children had just decided to stop the artificial ventilation that was keeping their beloved father's lungs pumping so that he could die in peace. I had been called to lead the family in prayer for their father at his bedside right after the extubation.

Amy and I arrived just as the tube was being removed. Although he looked more natural once the ventilator was removed, he still had not made any physical movements. With all the machinery turned off, it was very quiet in the ICU. No infernal beeping.

In that sacred space, time seemed to stand still. Mr. Jenkins was lying motionlessly on the clean white sheets, surrounded by his grieving loved ones. All was silent. Holy ground.

After letting the sanctity of the moment sink in, I began a short prayer ritual I have developed for such times. Knowing that Mr. Jenkins and his children were Christians, I began with a short prayer asking God to receive Mr. Jenkins into that special place prepared for him in God's house, where Mr. Jenkins would be reunited with his loved ones and with Jesus. I asked that God would welcome him to that place "where there is no more suffering or tears or crying or pain, where the old order of things is passed away and where everything is new." I then prayed that the Holy Spirit, the Comforter, would be with the family members, who'd already begun to grieve Mr. Jenkins's death.

At this point things got very interesting. The next part of the brief ritual, already agreed to by Mr. Jenkins's family, was that I would read a series of short phrases, and the family would respond to each one by saying, "We release you."

So I started, "Mr. Jenkins, in knowing that you have led a good and complete life . . ."

Mr. Jenkins's family responded, "We release you." But the rest of what happened in that moment was totally unscripted. As the family voiced, "We release you," Mr. Jenkins's whole body shook. Remember, Mr. Jenkins hadn't moved a muscle in three days. Honestly, I don't know if he shook or spasmed, but I assure you, every part of Mr. Jenkins that could move moved.

The family looked at me with wide eyes, raised eyebrows, and fear in their faces. Not knowing what to do and not wanting to create a disturbance in the ICU, I just continued on as if nothing unusual had happened.

"Mr. Jenkins, in knowing that we have cared for your total well-being . . ."

"We release you."

Once again, Mr. Jenkins's whole body vibrated.

As I read through the whole litany of release, every time the family said, "We release you," Mr. Jenkins's body shook, twitched, jerked, or spasmed.

I acted as if this sort of thing happened every day. Nothing unusual. I concluded the little ritual by reading Psalm 23, and as I finished the ritual by reading, "Surly goodness and mercy will follow me all the days of my life, and I will dwell in the house of the Lord, forever," Mr. Jenkins let out a long sustained final breath, and then the heart monitors in the ICU went flat. Mr. Jenkins gave up the ghost.

We all looked at one another in amazement at what had just taken place.

Amy and I went out to the floor to notify the nurses that Mr. Jenkins had died. Our leaving also gave the family some time alone with him to say their peace. As soon as we got out of earshot of Mr. Jenkins's family, Amy grabbed me with both hands and, with that look of a deer caught in the headlights, nearly screamed, "You gotta teach me how to do *that*!"

We sat down, and I explained that I had absolutely no idea what had just happened in that ICU room or why. We'd been given a prime demonstration that death is still mysterious. With all our medicines, monitors, and machinery, we have not been able to tame death. It comes in its own sweet time and its own sweet way. It is always unique, and everyone dies differently. There is no one way to do it.

After informing the nurses and filling out a little paperwork (no one is really dead in a hospital until the paperwork is completed), we felt we'd given the family enough time alone with Mr. Jenkins, so Amy and I went back to say goodbye. As we debriefed our shared experience, I was amazed to hear that what had taken place had been really comforting to the Jenkins family. All the shaking and then his dying as we finished the prayer made them feel that they'd made the right decision to stop the artificial breathing machinery; it was just his time to go.

Mayhem in the Morgue

■

Lord, what fools these mortals be!

—Shakespeare, Puck in *A Midsummer Night's Dream*

I'd no sooner been handed the on-call pager for the night when the phone rang in the chaplain's office. It was a long distance call on the outside line. The woman on the other end of the phone was clearly from the South—and obviously a little frantic.

As my ear became accustomed to her drawl, I realized she was asking for help in getting some hair. At first, I thought she was from out of town and needed directions to a beauty parlor, but as the conversation continued, I realized she was calling because she wanted hair from a man who'd just died at the hospital.

The dead man had been serving time in a local prison and had hanged himself. He'd been brought to the hospital in a vain effort to revive him. The woman on the phone was a former girlfriend who was trying to get Social Security benefits for their son, but to do so she had to prove paternity. For this, she needed some of the deceased man's hair. The problem was, the man had shaved his head, so this frantic woman with the New Orleans drawl was asking if I, the chaplain, would go retrieve some pubic hair from his dead body to send to her so that she could prove her son's paternity.

No way in hell.

As I was trying to explain that it was not in my job description to retrieve pubic hair from dead bodies, she tearfully implored, "But I need help . . . and you're supposed to help people, aren't you?" I looked to the ceiling, prayed for some divine intervention, and then noticed the pithy little framed platitude hanging on the wall over the phone: "What would Jesus do?" I realized to my dismay that Jesus would go get the damn pubic hair. I took her number and said I'd call her back when the deed was done.

Before trying to find out where the dead body had been taken, I made a mental note to stop by the switchboard operator's desk and provide a detailed tutorial on what calls should and should not be transferred to the chaplain's office.

The night was not beginning well.

After attending to a few minor chores, I headed off to locate our recently deceased prisoner. I was told that the body had been taken to the morgue and was awaiting pick up from the coroner's office. Hospital protocol requires that the coroner be notified whenever a person dies within twenty-four hours of being admitted.

The morgue is really just a big walk-in freezer. This is where the hospital stores bodies awaiting pickup by either a funeral home or, as in this case, the coroner. I'd been to the morgue only once before, and that was when I toured the hospital on my first day there.

Just as I was about to go down to the morgue, the pager went off with a call from staff in the Emergency Department. When I got to the ED, I was informed that the mother of another patient who'd died earlier that day had arrived and wanted to see her son's body. The grieving mother, who was in a wheelchair, was accompanied by two equally grief-stricken aunties. And the man they were looking for was also in the morgue. So, after a quick call to Security (after 5:00 p.m. they were the only ones with a key to the morgue), our little group headed down to the basement.

Of course, the narrow hallway to the morgue was grim, dimly lit, and more than a little spooky. The security guard did not look at all pleased to be there. I explained to the ladies that, since there were several bodies in the morgue, the guard and I would need to find their son and bring him to an outer room for viewing. Then the security guard opened the huge vault-like door, and he and I entered the room.

Once we got inside and the huge door was closed behind us, the security guard looked at me and whispered, "This place gives me the creeps." Trying to stay on task, we went in search of the ladies' loved one. I remember there were four or five bodies wrapped in black plastic bags and lying on gurneys. Attached to the bag's zippers were paper tags with identification information. I began to wonder which bag held the all-important pubic hair I would have to retrieve later, after the grieving women got to see their son.

The guard found the body we were looking for and suggested that we just unzip the bag down below his face for the ladies to view. That seemed like a good idea, since the man was very large—maybe six foot three and well over 250 pounds. Even with the gurney, the guard and I struggled in those cramped quarters to get the man into the small viewing area.

The guard was about to open the door and let the ladies in when I stopped him. Remembering that the mother was in a wheelchair, I thought it would be a good idea to lower the gurney so she could have a better view of her son. Although I'd never been properly trained on gurney mechanics, I figured, "How difficult can this be?" and pushed the foot level to lower the gurney. Apparently, I pushed the wrong lever. Instantly, the large man's feet went straight up and his head straight down. If not for the cat-like reflexes of the guard, I would have been in a world of hurt as the newly deceased 250-pound body would have slid off of the gurney and onto me.

The gurney was now at a 45-degree angle, and the guard was desperately holding on to the man's feet to keep him from sliding off. Freaking out, the guard screamed at me, "You better get this thing level fast before all the blood rushes to his head and it pops."

This was followed by shrieks of horror from three female voices in the dimly lit hallway on the other side of the morgue door.

We managed to get the gurney level again, and the rest of the activities in the viewing room with the three women who'd come in to grieve their loved one went off without a hitch. They were very grateful for our efforts. As I was escorting the mother in the wheelchair and her two sisters back down the dimly lit hallway, I could hear the security guard locking the huge door behind us and grumbling under his breath, "This place gives me the creeps."

One thing I did learn from that experience in the morgue was that there is still a God in heaven—because the body of the deceased prisoner with the highly coveted pubic hair had already been picked up by the coroner's office. Now they would have to help the frantic woman in New Orleans.

I also learned not to take myself too seriously. After all, we are just silly little people on a great big planet often just doing the best we can.

Soul Tsunami

■

The answer to the question of the preparation for this kind of work is that you learn the care of the dying from the dying themselves. But only if you look at them with respect and never merely with pity, and allow them to teach you. It is they who show us that the fear of death is overcome. Seeing this, we, too, can come to the place [where] . . . we cannot know what is beyond the end of our days, but we can enter into an order of things which can make us say, "I'm not afraid."

—Cicely Saunders

It started off just like any normal week. After a regular Monday at work I attended an evening bioethics lecture given by Dr. Sarah Shannon, an associate professor at the University of Washington's School of Nursing. A research specialist, Dr. Shannon shared a lot of statistical information about end-of-life issues in North America—information I found quite surprising. For example, she told us how it's only in the past sixty years that age-old understandings of death and dying have been radically altered. Starting in the 1950s with the intervention of heart and lung machines, then into the 1960s with CPR (cardio pulmonary resuscitation), dialysis, and organ transplants, what humanity had understood as death from time immemorial was now being postponed artificially by scientific means.

Additionally, she pointed out that most of the court cases involving medical ethics during the first thirty years since this death-defying revolution centered on hospitals and medical practitioners asking for legal help so that they might do all things possible to keep folks alive and postpone death, often against patient and familial desires. But in the 1980s, the tide started to shift, and the majority of legal battles became focused on getting the families of terminal patients to "let go" of their loved ones, suspending artificial interventions, and allowing nature to take its course. I suppose that the very limited quality of life for many of those receiving the heroic measures, the limited resources available, and the exorbitant costs involved all contributed to this change in thinking.

But what disturbed me about Dr. Shannon's presentation was a reference she made to a March 2009 article in the *Journal of the American Medical Association* (JAMA) highlighting a study of cancer patients that found that the most religious people in our society were the ones who wanted the most interventions at the end of life. According to the research, devout Christians are *more* likely than most other people to want everything humanly possible done in order to delay death.

The researchers in the JAMA study offered several theories as to why this is the case. Christians may believe that God will use the treatments to heal them; that God may miraculously cure them; that God may use the suffering to ensure a positive transformation; that it is immoral not to do everything possible; or, that giving in to death may be seen as giving up on God. The study concludes, "Failure to address the spiritual needs of terminal cancer patients could conceivably contribute to a spiritual crisis at the EOL (end of life), thereby leading to more aggressive care."

While I can see all these as possible explanations, my own suspicion is that devout Christians are more likely to want "everything done" because we are often the ones most afraid of dying. I base this belief on both my nine years of experience working as a hospice chaplain and my nearly twenty years as a traveling evangelist and pastor of an independent charismatic church. In recent years, I've been with more than one thousand people of various faith traditions who have died. My experience is that, of the folks I've been with who were most afraid of dying, at least half were outspoken evangelical Christians. This thought—that committed Christians are the ones who are most terrified of death—haunted me all week after I heard Dr. Shannon speak on Monday night.

Then came Friday. On Friday, I received word that one of my dearest and oldest friends had been tragically killed in a motorcycle accident. Tommy was a great husband and father, a wonderful worship leader, a good pastor, and one of the finest men I've ever known. He was the kind of man you hoped every minister would be—honest and compassionate. And his laugh . . . I'll always remember his laugh. It was loud and inviting.

It had been a beautiful sunny day, and Tom was driving to a nearby park to play with his family. The truck didn't see him on the motorcycle, and in an instant he was gone.

To be honest, I was also grieving the loss of our close brotherhood. For more than five years, Tommy and I had joined several other evangelical pastors for a few hours of prayer together every Tuesday. We went on mission trips together. We gave retreats together. But over the years, Tommy and I drifted apart not only in miles but also in theology. To be fair, the separation started when I broke faith by asserting that homosexuality is not a sin and that gay folks should be allowed to get married. Tom, on the other hand, continued in our shared conservative evangelical beliefs. We were living on opposite sides of the continent in more ways than one.

I was still reeling from the news of Tom's death when the tsunami of March 2011 hit Japan. I remember watching the storm's destruction and the ensuing nuclear meltdown in horror and disbelief. It felt like death was everywhere.

Where was God when my friend Tom died? Couldn't God have done something, stalled out the truck or something? And what about all those people in Japan? Why did they have to die? Why such misery? Am I really supposed to accept that most of the people in Japan have gone to hell to be tormented eternally while my friend Tom is in heaven simply based on what they chose to believe in the short span of their lives? Is this mercy? Is this the way a loving God would set up the game?

As I often do when I am in great pain, I retreated into my head. I spent the weekend reading Philippe Ariès's *The Hour of Our Death: The Classic History of Western Attitudes toward Death over the Last One Thousand Years*, searching for answers. According to his exhaustive research, Ariès asserts it's only been in the past seven hundred to eight hundred years that Western Christians have been afraid of death. Prior to that, they simply viewed it as a natural part of life. What caused this change? Ariès suggests the shift was the result of Christian preachers developing a new theology about heaven or hell, who is in and who is out.[42]

DISTURBING THE COMFORTABLE

Several years ago, a young man named Rob Bell wrote a book called *Love Wins* that inspired a lot of controversy among evangelicals. Bell's book begins with the following story.

> Several years ago we had an art show at our church. I had been giving a series of teachings on peacemaking, and we invited artists to display their paintings, poems, and sculptures that reflected their understanding of what it means to be a peacemaker. One woman included in her work a quote from Mahatma Gandhi, which a number of people found quite compelling.
>
> But not everyone.
>
> Someone attached a piece of paper to it. On the piece of paper was written: "Reality check: He's in hell."
>
> Really?
>
> Gandhi's in hell?
>
> He is?
>
> We have confirmation of this?
>
> Somebody knows this?
>
> Without a doubt?
>
> And that somebody decided to take on the responsibility of letting the rest of us know?[43]

Bell's book created quite a stir in the evangelical community because he was questioning these centuries-old understandings of who gets into heaven and who goes to hell. His questions, which challenged the meta-narrative we have lived under in North America since our country's beginnings, lanced the deep-seated fear tucked away in the unspoken closet of belief of many conservative Christians. As a hospital chaplain, I meet this fear in patients and family members on a daily basis: Does God *really* love me?

This fear is based, in no small measure, on a sermon preached by another American pastor, Jonathan Edwards, on July 8, 1741, in a little Congregational church in Enfield, Connecticut. Edwards verbalized his now famous image of "Sinners in the Hands of an Angry God," an image that haunts many faith-filled believers to this very day. Edwards preached in part . . .

> The God that holds you over the pit of hell, much as one holds a spider, or some loathsome insect over the fire, abhors you, and is dreadfully provoked: his wrath towards you burns like fire; he looks upon you as worthy of nothing else, but to be cast into the fire; he is of purer eyes than to bear to have you in his sight; you are ten thousand times more abominable in his eyes, than the most hateful venomous serpent is in ours. You have offended him infinitely more than ever a stubborn rebel did his prince; and yet it is nothing but his hand that holds you from falling into the fire every moment.[44]

That sermon not only helped spark the First Great Awakening,[45] it also helped cement a deep fear that the God of the Bible cannot be trusted.

Now, lest you think that Jonathan Edwards and his sermon are just archaic relics of our distant past, think again. Many conservative evangelical pastors, preachers, and teachers still consider Edwards to be the greatest theologian to spring from American soil. The sentiments that form the basis of his sermon are still foundational to the belief system of many evangelicals today.

Every week I encounter patients or family members who are desperately afraid that they or their loved ones are going to spend an eternity of torment in hell unless I can somehow magically get them "saved." In fact, many who do believe they are "saved" remain frightened by the prospect that they have not done enough to please this "angry God." These dear folks may proclaim a salvation by grace but they live a salvation by works. They believe their salvation depends not only on doing good deeds to appease God but also on believing all the right things about God in all the right ways. Additionally, these God-fearing believers often feel they are carrying on their hands the blood of any loved one who doesn't give his or her life to Jesus before dying. It is simply terrifying.

This reality became evident for me as I watched my friend Tommy's funeral streaming live on the Internet. It was a beautiful ceremony with numerous people heaping well-deserved accolades on my friend. But the underlying message was that we'd all better come to the same belief Tommy professed, or else we'll fry forever.

Tom's memorial service unleashed my own emotional tsunami. On one hand I was grieving the loss of a wonderful man and the close friendship we'd once enjoyed. But I was also grieving the loss of a certain kind of faith I'd once had, a faith that had carried me into many a room like the one where his memorial service was held, rooms packed with hundreds of people all worshiping God passionately and fervently, with a deep expectation that God would show up in some manifest way and perform miracles or speak to us. I spent many years attending meetings like this and, in all honesty, I have witnessed miracles. I have been overwhelmed by the magnificent presence of an almighty and all-loving God. In these contexts I have enjoyed incredible friendships and deep bonds of fellowship that have been very life-giving. I dearly miss that particular style of worship music, which I find so emotionally evocative. But the message that is often declared in such settings, a message of hellfire and damnation, gives me the willies.

After Tom's memorial service, I sat in my bedroom and cried for hours. I cried for the years I'd spent on my massive ego trip and arrogant assurance of things beyond my understanding. I cried for my part in the hypocrisy often played out in presentations from the pulpit that were so disconnected from the reality of the lives of the preachers. I cried for the downright meanness that characterized our talk about any with a different belief system than those of us who claim to know the Way, the Truth, and the Life. I cried for all the years I spent heaping fear and guilt on people who didn't share my beliefs, for all the time and energy I'd invested in spreading such an obscene image of an angry God.

For the next week I was tired and forgetful. I had no mental focus. Making decisions at work was impossible because I felt mentally paralyzed. I had no appetite and walked around with a deep sadness, bursting into tears without warning. It felt like I was crawling out of my skin.

During that week following Tom's accident and the great Japanese tsunami, I wrestled with Ariès, Bell, Edwards, and my own demons and fears concerning my life choices. Death does that. It causes those who survive to reflect on who we are, how we're living, and what gives meaning to our lives.

I contemplated the awful damage that's been done in the name of God for nearly a millennium by Christian preachers, myself included, who have hijacked the Good News of God's grace with the twisted message of God's judgment. I faced the dirty little secret that it's pretty easy to amass power and money if I can convince you there is a wonderful place called heaven where you'll find beauty, safety, and acceptance but there's also another place called hell where you'll experience torment, suffering, and unending pain—and I hold the only key to that good place. Such a magic key is worth a lot of money and power.

But the crazy thing is, how do we really know who holds this magic key? *Christianity Today* has reported that there are now more than thirty-seven thousand different Christian denominations,[46] all proclaiming "Follow us because we are the true path." Which one of these thirty-seven thousand groups really knows the way in?

And what about all those fallen preachers who told us they had the magic key before they slept with someone they shouldn't have, or stole money, or raped children? They claimed to know how to please this angry caricature of God, they made lots of money selling tapes and books on how to behave in ways that would appease this judgmental God, then they couldn't live up to their own teachings.

But the really insidious aspect to this whole spiritual charade is that deep down, many of us simply do not like ourselves—so we buy into this contemptible lie that God doesn't like us either. And we're hooked.

COMFORTING THE DISTURBED

Noted psychiatrist Gerald May has sadly observed, "I have yet to meet a person in modern western culture who was not in some way cruelly self-abusive."[47]

May's quote reminds me of Charlie. Charlie was a devout Christian, a weekly attendee at church. Charlie had owned and operated several successful small businesses and had a loving wife as well as several children and grandchildren. Charlie loved to tease people, but there was a distinct edge to his teasing. As I got to know him, he told me about how he hated his father. His father had been an alcoholic who would drink away his paycheck, so Charlie had to go to work at age fourteen to help support the family. As a result, Charlie never graduated from high school and carried that shame the rest of his life. Charlie had always loved airplanes and dreamed of becoming a pilot, but because he had no high school diploma, his dreams never became a reality. So for more than seventy years, Charlie carried that hatred for his father and clung to a self-narrative that he was inferior because he hadn't graduated from high school.

As I've shared earlier, we are all formed by the stories we tell ourselves. Our behavior is deeply influenced by the narratives we choose to live by. For Charlie, the narrative that he was a failure due to his lack of formal education fueled an angry soul. Often it would manifest itself in a playful teasing, but if you crossed the line, as his children knew all too well, the wrath of Charlie's deep self-hatred would emerge in full force.

For example, Charlie loved to tell a story of an evening when he and his wife and some friends were going to dinner at a nearby busy restaurant and found parking was at a premium. After Charlie finally located an empty space, just as he was about to pull in, another car quickly pulled into the spot Charlie wanted. The driver in the other car then committed the unforgivable sin by smiling at Charlie as if to say, "Beat you!"

Charlie stewed over that smile all through the appetizer, and then quietly excused himself from the dinner table. He went outside and let the air out of all four of the other guy's tires, and then went back in to finish dinner with his friends. As they were leaving the restaurant, they saw a tow truck hooking up the other guy's car as the driver scratched his head in disbelief. Charlie loved to tell about how, as he pulled out of the parking lot, "I smiled and waved goodbye to him."

Charlie's experience of this angry God of Christianity only reinforced his tormenting self-narrative. There are winners and losers. Winners are saved, and losers go to hell. It's us versus them. As a result, my friend Charlie died a very painful death. The years of pent-up anger were bursting through his social filters and he nearly alienated everyone who really loved him.

But Charlie isn't the only person I think of when I read Gerald May's quote. The quote also reminds me of myself. Like Charlie, I have deep wounds of failure and shame, but, mercifully, the Jesus I've encountered along my journey is one who has helped me dismantle my self-hating narrative. At my lowest, most shame-filled moments of self-loathing, the grace-giving compassionate One has always been there to forgive me, love me, accept me, and heal me. Always.

And I am not alone. As I have studied the Gospels, the Jesus portrayed there actually never rejected anyone. He ate with oppressors and oppressed alike. There were no "ins" and "outs" with the biblical Jesus. This is not to say there weren't people who annoyed him. But the only accounts I know of where Jesus really got mad is when folks claimed to hold the magic key that would open the door to God for them but would exclude anyone who wasn't like them (see Matthew 23).

One of the main lessons I've learned from my time serving the dying is that we're all in this together. All the distinctions and categories we create to define the "other" are an illusion. We're all frightened neurotic beings desperately seeking a place to fit and find someone to love us. My favorite quote is from my hero, Thomas Merton, who wrote, "Thank God, thank God that I *am* like other men." Merton recognized, after spending more than twenty-five years trying to make himself perfect while sequestered behind the wall of a Cistercian monastery, that he was just as crazy and neurotic and messed up as everybody else—and that insight was liberating! It's as if all of humanity is one big twelve-step group, and because we are flawed—we fit.

We all have dreams, and hopes, and fears.

We all die.

We all need grace.

We are all in this together. But there's more. Not only are we all in the same boat together, but we can be assured that God is here with us. The biblical text I share with the dying more often than any other is from the letter to the Hebrews:

> Let your character or moral disposition be free from love of money (including greed, avarice, lust, and craving for earthly possessions) and be satisfied with your present circumstances and with what you have; for [God] has said, I will not in any way fail you nor give you up nor leave you without support. I will not, I will not, I will not in any degree leave you helpless nor forsake nor let you down (relax My hold on you)! Assuredly not! (Hebrews 13:5 AMP)

This is not the "angry God" of Jonathan Edwards who causes fear and torment, but the *Abba* of Jesus who offers acceptance, unconditional love, and grace. The good news I have discovered is this God of grace, who will not desert or forsake us, works continuously to dismantle my negative self-narratives, the myths about myself that add to my suffering. In the midst of the rejections, wounds, and disappointments of my life, the God I have encountered along my journey whispers that I am Beloved. Gives grace. Offers loving acceptance. Henri Nouwen wrote in his journal:

> Am I afraid to die? I am every time I let myself be seduced by the noisy voices of my world telling me that my "little life" is all I have and advising me to cling to it with all my might. But when I let those voices move to the background of my life and listen to that small soft voice calling me the Beloved, I know that there is nothing to fear and that dying is the greatest act of love, the act that leads me into the eternal embrace of my God whose love is everlasting.[48]

I've also learned that this whisper of grace calls for response on my part. Will I trust that ineffable voice whispering in the silence or will I trust the self-limiting narrative in my mind? If I answer "Yes" to that whisper, then as Charles de Foucauld warns, "The one thing we owe absolutely to God is never to be afraid of anything."[49]

If you've followed me thus far, you've probably noticed that I'm rather inconsistent. But if you'll remember, as my friend Jack taught me, I believe consistency is overrated. The tension I wrestle with daily is how to live passionately as a follower of Jesus—seeking to live in ways that are not passive, self-centered, or fearful of life—and yet hold it all lightly, recognizing that my understanding of what it means to follow Jesus could be totally wrong.

MORE GRACE

I drove out to Applegate Lake earlier this week to meet a very kind man who is fighting esophageal cancer. Joe and his wife have been living in their fifth-wheel trailer for the past four years so they could enjoy the surrounding beauty of the Siskiyou Mountains. He told me, "Being on hospice scares the hell out of me." Joe told me that he loved his wife, his life, and fishing too much to die just now. After I explained that the goal of hospice is to help folks like him be as active, pain-free, and best able to enjoy however many moments they have for as long as they have, he relaxed a little.

On the drive back to town after my visit with Joe, I pulled to the side of the road. The sky was blue; the sun was high; and the car thermometer said the outside temperature was 79 degrees. I pulled out the canvas camping chair I keep in the trunk for just such occasions and stopped simply to enjoy the beauty surrounding me. The mountains were still lush green from the spring rains. The lavender by the side of the road was in bloom. The cool breeze caused the small leaves of the manzanita bushes to shiver while the dark gnarly trunks remained unmoved. The capped peaks rising above the Applegate were so serene, they just invited me to sit a spell.

As I sat there, I prayed for Joe, and I thought about many of the folks whose stories I have shared with you in this book. I am so grateful for the joy of having known them and for what they've taught me about becoming a compassionate human being. I'm so grateful for my loving wife, who has taught me to be kind, and my counter-cultural son, who makes me laugh. And I'm so grateful for Jesus, who interrupted my life more than forty years ago. I love him as much today as on the day we met, but I have to confess I feel I know less about him now than I did then. I have more questions than answers, but in a strange way I am much happier than I've ever been. For much of my life, I've felt like a round peg being shoved into a square hole, but somehow, I seem to fit here. And I'm grateful.

I know I've raised issues that require larger minds than my own to be sorted out. In the meantime, I am very content to live in my little part of the world, serving the folks God entrusts to my care, and continuing to prospect for grace.

Just yesterday we admitted a new hospice patient who has been battling ALS since last summer. He is young, warm, has a loving family and a great sense of humor. Theirs is an immensely grace-filled home. I'll hang out with folks like them, and Joe, providing a little support where I can, and hopefully together we'll all become a little more human. In the course of my travels, I have discovered, as the great Sufi sage Rumi wrote several hundred years ago: *"I need more grace than I thought."*

And so, my friend, the time has come for us to part. I thank you for spending this time with me and allowing me to share stories of the wonderful folks I've met along my journey. I truly hope they will help you as you follow your own path. In parting, I'd like to share a blessing I often use at life celebration services. If I knew who wrote it, I'd give credit—but I do not. Here goes.

Life is short.
And we do not have too much time
to gladden the hearts
of those who travel this way with us.
So make haste to love.
Be swift to be kind.
And may the Divine Mystery
who is beyond our ability to know completely,
but who created us,
and loves us,
and travels this way with us,
bless us and grant us peace.

Epilogue

■

Ministry means the ongoing attempt to put one's own search for God, with all the moments of pain and joy, despair and hope, at the disposal of those who want to join this search but do not know how.

—Henri Nouwen, *Creative Ministry*

I am often asked what is it I do as a hospice chaplain. My answer usually depends on how much time I have to spend with the questioner.

My short, elevator-ride-length reply is "I work to make a safe place for people to go crazy." When a doctor has just told you that you're soon going to die, how should you respond? My goal is to help create a safe place for patients and their loved ones who have just received this awful news to go crazy, without harming themselves or others. That's the quick answer.

The longer, more complete version of my response goes something like this. Before seeing patients, I try to center myself by connecting to God—and for me, this connection happens through my relationship with Jesus. My desire is to offer loving acceptance (grace) to the folks I serve. To do so, I need to refill regularly, because I leak. I generally try to avoid hearing the diagnosis a patient has received before I meet him or her, so as to allow the human being I meet to introduce herself or himself to me on her or his own terms. For example, I don't want to meet Joe, the cancer patient. I want to meet Joe, the 49ers fan who always has a piece of candy and a hug for his granddaughter.

During the visit, I try to listen to my patient with my whole self. I seek to avoid hurrying, instead practicing what the Zen folks call mindfulness. When I am with a patient, I try not to think about the charting I need to do or what I will have for lunch. I want to honor each person by listening to him or her with my whole being. Some folks want to talk about what's going on with them, so we talk about that. Other folks want a vacation from what is happening to them, so we goof around. For those who are uncommunicative, I make it a point to spend at least twenty minutes just watching them and silently praying for them in a way that honors their faith background (if I know it). I give each individual my full attention because I want to honor the life of the person before me, even if that person cannot communicate with me. I want every person to matter—to be really seen.

Often, this is hard. Today, I sat with a man named George at a skilled nursing facility. He was lying on his bed, his hands shaking and his eyes open, but totally uncommunicative. He's trapped in a body that no longer works. George is a few years younger than I am. He has led a very active life, and was a councilman for many years in his hometown. This once vibrant community mover and shaker is now lying on a bed in a nursing home with no one to notice him. No more power lunches. No more planning committee meetings. Just day after day of lying on a bed, staring at the ceiling.

As I sat there silently praying for him, I realized that one day I might be lying on a similar bed somewhere, waiting my turn to die. George, by his very presence, invites me to face my own finitude. As I prayed for George, I also prayed for myself. I prayed that when I got home I would make sure to tell my wife how beautiful she is and how much I love her, and to thank her for helping make me a kinder, gentler human being. I prayed I would tell my son how proud I am of him and not let social convention keep me from lavishing him with love. And I prayed I wouldn't bitch about having to walk Finch (our beloved Westie); that instead I'd be grateful I still have two good legs that work when I ask them to.

Notes

■ ■ ■

1. Joan Borysenko, quoted in *Living with Grief: Before and After the Death*, ed. Kenneth J. Doka, "Lessons before Dying" by Joyce Davidson (Washington, DC: Hospice Foundation of America, 2007), 308.

2. "Satori may be defined as an intuitive looking into the nature of things in contradistinction to the analytical or logical understanding of it. Practically, it means the unfolding of a new world hitherto unperceived in the confusion of a dualistically trained mind . . . the opening of satori is the remaking of life itself." D. T. Suzuki, *Zen Buddhism*, ed. William Barrett (New York: Doubleday, 2006), 98–99.

3. Nikos Kazantzakis, *Zorba the Greek* (New York: Simon & Schuster, 1952), 120–21.

4. Aleksandar Hemon, "The Aquarium: A Tale of Two Daughters," *The New Yorker,* June 13, 2011, 62.

5. Ibid., 59.

6. Æschylus, quoted by Robert F. Kennedy, "Remarks on the Assassination of Martin Luther King, Jr.," http://www.americanrhetoric.com/speeches/rfkonmlkdeath.html (accessed March 23, 2013).

7. Suzuki, *Zen Buddhism*, 6–7.

8. Joseph Campbell and Bill Moyers, *The Power of Myth* (New York: Doubleday, 1988), 39.

9. Anne Lamott, *Traveling Mercies: Some Thoughts on Faith* (New York: Anchor Books, 1999), 143.

10. Margaret Mohrmann, *Medicine as Ministry* (Cleveland: Pilgrim Press, 1995), 69.

11. C. S. Lewis, *The Voyage of the Dawn Treader* (New York: Collier Books, 1970), 1.

12. Ibid., 90–91.

13. Campbell and Moyers, *Power of Myth*,150.

14. Kevin Prosch, "Kiss the Son," ©1994 Integrity's Hosanna! Music 7th Time Music (Admin. by Integrity Music, Inc.), CCLI song #1514879.

15. Ibid.

16. Henri Nouwen, *Bread for the Journey: A Daybook of Wisdom and Faith* (San Francisco: HarperSanFrancisco, 1997), January 25.

17. Thomas Moore, *Care of the Soul* (New York: HarperPerennial, 1992), 20.

18. Thomas Merton, *A Year with Thomas Merton: Daily Mediations from His Journals* (New York: HarperOne, 2004), 81.

19. Moore, *Care of the Soul,* 136.

20. Karl Rahner, *Prayers and Meditations: An Anthology of the Spiritual Writings of Karl Rahner,* ed. John Griffiths (New York: Seabury Press, 1980), 26.

21. This insight was presented to me in a lecture by Dr. Sam Storms, a Presbyterian minister.

22. Miguel de Unamuno, quoted in Ernest Kurtz and Katherine Ketcham, *The Spirituality of Imperfection: Storytelling and the Search for Meaning* (New York: Bantam Books, 2002), 204.

23. Belden Lane, *The Solace of Fierce Landscapes* (New York: Oxford University Press, 2007), 35.

24. Parker Palmer, *A Hidden Wholeness* (San Francisco: Jossey-Bass, 2004), 58–59.

25. Richard Foster, *Celebration of Discipline: The Path to Spiritual Growth* (San Francisco: HarperSanFrancisco, 1988), 130.

26. Moore, *Care of the Soul,* 51.

27. Marc Gafni, *Soul Prints: Your Path to Fulfillment* (New York: Fireside, 2001), 79.

28. Antony the Great, quoted in *The Little Book of Hours: Praying with the Community of Jesus* (Brewster, MA: Paraclete Press, 2003), 193.

29. Robert Solomon, "Lecture 16: Heidegger on the World and the Self," *No Excuses: Existentialism and the Meaning of Life* (Chantilly, VA: The Teaching Company, CD, 2000).

30. David Biro, *The Language of Pain: Finding Words, Compassion, and Relief*, 1st ed. (New York: W.W. Norton, 2010), 153.

31. John J. Pilch, *Healing in the New Testament: Insights from Medical and Mediterranean Anthropology* (Minneapolis: Fortress Press, 2000).

32. Ibid., 34.

33. Henri Nouwen, *Mornings with Henri J. M. Nouwen: Readings and Reflections* (Cincinnati: Servant Books, 2005), 106.

34. Gary Smalley and John Trent, *The Gift of the Blessing* (New York: Inspirational Press, 1993).

35. Quoted in John Piper, *Desiring God* (Sisters, OR: Multnomah Press, 1996), 211.

36. Nouwen, *Mornings*, 106.

37. Henri Nouwen, *Seeds of Hope: A Henri Nouwen Reader* (New York: Image Books, 1997), 180–81.

38. Thich Nhat Hanh, *Chanting from the Heart: Buddhist Ceremonies and Daily Practice* (Berkeley, CA: Parallax Press, 2007), 41.

39. Deng Ming-Dao, *365 Tao: Daily Meditations* (New York: HarperOne, 1992), "158. Dying."

40. Joan Chittister, *Scarred by Struggle, Transformed by Hope* (Grand Rapids, MI: William B. Eerdmans, 2003), 95.

41. Ibid, 71.

42. Philippe Ariès's *The Hour of Our Death: The Classic History of Western Attitudes toward Death over the Last One Thousand Years* (New York: Alfred A. Knopf, 1981).

43. Rob Bell, *Love Wins: A Book about Heaven, Hell, and the Fate of Every Person Who Ever Lived* (New York: HarperCollins, 2011), 1–2.

44. Jonathan Edwards, *Sinners in the Hands of an Angry God* (Phillipsburg, NJ: P&R Publishing, 1992), 22–23.

45. The First Great Awakening was a massive revival that took place in the American colonies from about 1730 to 1760 and led to thousands of conversions to a Protestant Reformation view of Christianity.

46. Timothy George, "Is Christ Divided?" *Christianity Today* (2005, July), retrieved April 22, 2008 from http://www.ctlibrary.com/ct/2005/july/23.31.html.

47. Gerald May, quoted in Brennan Manning, *Ruthless Trust: The Ragamuffin's Path to God* (San Francisco: HarperSanFrancisco, 2000), 155–56.

48. Henri Nouwen, *Mornings,* 107.

49. Charles de Foucauld, quoted in Brennan Manning, *The Furious Longing of God* (Colorado Springs: David Cook, 2009), 112.

Bibliography

■ ■ ■

Jalal al-Din, Rumi, transl. Coleman Barks, with John Moyne. T*he Essential Rumi,* reprint ed. San Francisco: HarperOne, 2004.

Jalal al-Din, Rumi, transl. Coleman Barks. *The Soul of Rumi: A New Collection of Ecstatic Poems.* 1st ed. San Francisco: HarperSanFrancisco, 2001.

Kurtz, Ernest, and Katherine Ketcham. *The Spirituality of Imperfection: Modern Wisdom from Classic Stories.* New York: Bantam Books, 1992.

Lane, Belden C. *The Solace of Fierce Landscapes: Exploring Desert and Mountain Spirituality.* Oxford and New York: Oxford University Press, 2007.

Merton, Thomas. *Conjectures of a Guilty Bystander.* 1st ed. Garden City, NY: Image, 1968.

———. *New Seeds of Contemplation.* Shambhala Library. Boston: Shambhala, 2003.

Moore, Thomas. *Care of the Soul: A Guide for Cultivating Depth and Sacredness in Everyday Life.* 1st ed. New York: HarperCollins, 1992.

Nouwen, Henri J. M. *Bread for the Journey: A Daybook of Wisdom and Faith.* 1st ed. San Francisco: Harper SanFrancisco, 1997.

Nouwen, Henri J. M., and Robert Durback. *Seeds of Hope: A Henri Nouwen Reader.* Toronto and New York: Bantam Books, 1989.

Palmer, Parker J. *A Hidden Wholeness: The Journey toward an Undivided Life.* 1st ed. San Francisco: Jossey-Bass, 2008.

Reynolds, Barbara. *Dante: The Poet, the Political Thinker, the Man.* 1st Shoemaker & Hoard ed. Emeryville, CA: Shoemaker & Hoard. Distributed by Publishers Group West, 2006.

Rohr, Richard. *Falling Upward: A Spirituality for the Two Halves of Life.* 1st ed. San Francisco: Jossey-Bass, 2011.

Vanier, Jean. *Encountering "the Other."* New York: Paulist Press, 2005.

Whyte, David. *River Flow: New & Selected Poems 1984–2007.* Langley, WA: Many Rivers Press, 2007.